To my Dad who taught me countless things – some more useful than others – but most importantly to live life fully. I know you would have loved what I'm doing. I miss you every day.

Contents

So, You're Moving to France?	5
Paperwork & Bureaucracy: France's True National Sport	15
Finding a Home: A Full-Time Job with a Side of Mystery	35
Everyday Life: Learning the French Way	47
Language Struggles: The French You Never Learned in School	91
Culture & Traditions: Embracing the French Way	107
Final Thoughts: Are You Sure You Want to Stay?	133

So, You're Moving to France?

"Wait… you're moving to rural France? At 40? Away from your family, your friends, **leaving your entire life**? WHY?"

The reactions ranged from confusion to horror, I think my mother thought I was deserting her and she'd never see me again. Some assumed I was having a midlife crisis. It was a knee-jerk idea or pipedream, forgotten as quickly as spoken.

For the record, **it was none of those things**.

I sit here today writing this book, 12 months on. Partly to reflect on what it's taken to get here. Partly so I don't forget the funny things I've learnt (often the hard way). And hoping by sharing this, I might provide some hope to those embarking on the same rollercoaster of a journey, maybe even offer some laughs along the way.

So let me introduce us. We're Marie and Tom—two fairly normal (questionable) people who, like many Brits, spent years dreaming about packing up and escaping to France.

Tom's a practical, outdoorsy type who thrives on adventure. I, on the other hand, prefer my activities to involve some 'measured risk', eating good food, low levels of physical exertion, and a vodka and coke in hand. We balance each other out.

Our family (at the time) was complete with Belle, a typically stubborn, but comical Frenchie who genuinely believes she's a human. Complete with sulking behaviour if she can't sleep in our bed, share our dinner and sit on the front seat of the car. Although full disclosure - I may have played a **small** role in these delusions of grandeur by spoiling her rotten.

I'd spent my childhood family holidays exploring the West coast of France. Fond memories of long yellow sandy beaches, fringed with pine forests. Exploring old towns, stunning architecture where you feel like you're in the old Renault clio advert.. You know the one..

"Nicole?"

"Papa!?"

In later years I'd been travelling back to France to 'brush up' on my school French and even tentatively searching some job boards, dreaming of what could be.

My dad had passed away suddenly a few years previously, a stark reminder of how short life is. Approaching 40, friends were married off and settling down to have children but I had itchy feet.

Then I met Tom.

Coincidentally, Tom had spent most of his childhood in the same sort of area of France as I had. His parents had bought a holiday home there 30 odd years before. He'd always loved France too and had taken the plunge to move there wisely sorting his residency status (some pre-brexit foresight) a few years before.

It was crazy how aligned we were on everything, and our paths crossing at that time, felt like fate.

We were both fortunate to work remotely. So, we began hopping back and forth between France and the UK, forever doing the calculations to ensure I was within the 90/180-day Brex-shit rule. Friends thought we were **living the dream**:

- Chasing the weather
- Long lazy lunches in the sun.
- Fresh croissants every morning.

And sure, it was great—except for the soul-destroying back and forth, that feeling of limbo, and the slow realisation that the UK was no longer starting to feel like home. England became a place where we just caught up with family and friends, and counted down the days until we could get back to France.

So we talked. And then talked some more until one day, we just thought: Sod it. **Let's do it**.

Going somewhere on holiday is so different to living somewhere all year round. We didn't want to keep moving, and wanted to be sure on where we wanted to actually settle. So we even did a few house-sits so we could explore different parts of France too (No less than 5 star reviews on Trusted House Sitters I might add).

We landed on the beautiful Charente Maritime, on the South West Coast.

Just a little further South from where Tom was living previously.

Whilst still pretty rural, there was **a bit** more going on (we were only just in our 40's after all).

It was both close to the coast, and had reasonable transport links if we needed to get back to the UK.

Perfect.

Now all I had to do was get a visa. **How hard could that be?**

The Romantic Dream vs. The Bureaucratic Nightmare

I had a master's degree and over 20 years of experience in business. Australia with their tough immigration points system would welcome me in with open arms, so surely France would be delighted to have me?

As it turns out. **Absolutely not**.

France, you see, does not believe in making things easy. Unlike Spain or Portugal, which have embraced digital nomad visas, France still treats remote working with deep suspicion. Working for a French company wasn't an option either—unless they could prove that no single person in the entire country could possibly do the job I was applying for.

My French wasn't quite up to scratch either. I'd built a career in the corporate world of financial services – full of acronyms and terminology designed to make outsiders think those within it know more than they do! Full of management drivel that's all about 'leveraging synergies' and 'taking things offline' – it's as pretentious as it is vague. I mean, it's bad enough in English, let alone another language.

So I did what any rational person would do:

1. **Spent hours on government websites** (which totally contradicted each other and were filled with warnings around non-compliance).

2. **Paid an immigration lawyer** who smiled politely, shrugged, and said *"Pas possible."*. And happily produced the invoice for 500 euros. Helpful.

3. **Scrolled through Facebook expat groups**, where half the people were offering helpful advice, and glimmers of hope, and the other half were having nervous breakdowns about failed visa applications or rejected residency permits.

The more I searched, the clearer it became:

- If you were retired or didn't need to work, straight through.
- If you could prove some ancestral link e.g. French grandparents, you're all good
- If you had a giant pile of cash and were planning to run a gîte business that already had proven income, a few extra checks needed, but fairly straightforward
- Irish passport? Now you're laughing. Come to the front of the queue my friend, you don't even need a stamp.

I of course, was none of these things. I did briefly consider pretending to be, but I suspected that I would crumble under the slightest scrutiny.

The Breakthrough (or: How I Sold My Soul to Bureaucracy)

Eventually, after 12 months of blockers and knock backs, I found the solution: a *portage salarial*—a weird but wonderful French umbrella company that would act as my employer, advertise my job, and sweet-talk the French government into giving me a work permit.

Of course they take a nice slice for the pleasure of doing so, and whilst not the most straightforward option to set up, or lucrative long-term, with everything in balance it gave the most probable chance of visa success.

I was running with it.

The visa application itself was a classic French test of patience. Lots of paperwork to be expected, but no clear list of what's really needed. I was digging out my GCSE certificates and bank statements from 10 years ago for god's sake.

The appointment was then set for a trip to the French consulate in London. When you live in Devon, this is a bit of a faff.

The appointment went pretty smoothly really, I was well-prepared. That was until they rejected my passport photo because a single strand of hair was covering my eyebrow.

Cue a frantic dash around to a photo booth to get another. The problem with this, I'd been strategic – I knew this was coming.

My previous photos had been taken in the height of summer – a nice glow to the skin, light dusting of make-up, hair au-naturel - and all very Français. In that photo, I was looking my best.

The problem now: it was January. It was cold, I was pale, and I was still carrying my post-Christmas weight. That deeply unflattering photo was now going to be used on every piece of French paperwork for the rest of my life. ***Super!***

However, a few weeks later, the passport arrived—visa attached. Bad photo quickly forgotten. **We were officially moving to France.**

The Honeymoon Phase

I set off at the end of January, ready to start our new life.

Flashing immigration the biggest smile as they stamped my visa at Caen.

I needed to get my paperwork and inventory stamped to avoid me having to pay import tax on all my belongings – after all I still had a whole house full to bring over at some point - but no-one from customs was there?

Of course not. I mean, why would they be? It's 8am, and a large ferry of passengers are arriving from the UK, but you guys turn up to work when you're ready.

I was told by the friendly chap at immigration, I just needed to contact my local douanes.

"*C'est pas grave*" he said, (meaning it's not serious).

This is a phrase the French use freely, but as it turns out you shouldn't always believe them!

But for now, I was in.

The 5 hour drive down flew by as I listened to my French café jazz. Excited to see Tom and Belle as they'd gone ahead a few weeks before.

And I can tell you, the first few weeks were **blissful**. Every meal was delicious, every interaction felt charming, and every sunset looked like a postcard.

We breathed a sigh of relief when we arrived. Just chilled for a month or so and enjoyed it… then the real fun began.

But that's a story for another chapter…

Paperwork & Bureaucracy: France's True National Sport

OFII: The first immigration hurdle

Ah the OFII (*L'Office français de l'immigration et de l'intégration*) appointment – a thrilling bureaucratic rite of passage for anyone moving to France. If you thought getting your visa was **the hard part, surprise!**

Now you must prove you're willing to integrate, by attending a 3-4 hour *rendez-vouz* during which time you will

1. Take a language test to assess your French skills
2. Have an interview with an OFII officer, and
3. Sign an integration contract, promising to embrace French culture.

The exam tests for A1 level French, so just enough skills to be able to introduce yourself and buy a baguette without causing a major incident.

The written part was simple enough. The oral section was more nerve wracking. I passed though and was deemed above level A2. Wooohoo, all those hours spent on Duolingo were paying off!

Then you sit down with the OFII officer who asks a few more questions. This is to check you understand what you're signing up to, and if you need any extra help.

I probably understood about 60% of what was being said.

Then it's time to arrange where and when you're going to complete your civic training.

After this, you sign the *'contrat d'intégration républicaine'* – a formal pledge to integrate into French life. It basically means:

- You agree to respect French values

- You will try your best to integrate
- You acknowledge that bureaucracy will now be a permanent part of your existence.

It's serious business, but to be honest, if you've made it this far you're already pretty committed.

This contract, you're told, is a very important document, and required for visa renewals. Therefore you must keep a copy somewhere safe and absolutely not use it to light the wood burner etc.

You walk out, a little dazed, but one step closer to being a fully integrated resident of France. All you have to do now is survive the rest of the paperwork, *D'accord*?

The Medical

When you're coming to live in France and benefit from the healthcare, you can expect a compulsory medical examination, complete with chest x-ray.

I arrived for the *rendez-vous*, and no sooner had I sat in the waiting room, I was efficiently called up. The technician confirmed my details, ushered me into a cubicle and blurted something in (typically) lightning-speed French.

Way too fast – *pas compris*.

I understood to remove clothes, but missed the last bit.. I don't want to look stupid, so what do I do? I respond '*D'accord*' (ok), of course.

I start undressing, I'm now stood in my underwear. Hmmm how far should I go? I think.

Ok, logic tells you it's a chest X-ray, so the metal underwired bra is whipped off. But my pants?? I go with it, and walk as confidently as I can out from the cubicle, naked as baby.

I get a raised eyebrow from the technician and I just know it. **I've screwed up**.

I'm told to stand by the machine, I breathe in, 'click', breathe out 'click'.

And with that I'm told to go and get dressed. So I shamefully return to the cubicle, where my pants and dignity lay weeping in the corner. Five minutes later, I'm being handed my envelope complete with x-ray. I smile but avoid eye contact with technician. I inwardly hope our paths never cross again and scuttle off up the corridor to see the doctor.

The Doctor skimmed my file.

'Buvez-vous de l'alcool?' she asked.

I live in France now, the home of wine. What is the correct answer to this?

'Uh, *oui*'

She **nodded approvingly**, *'Tres bien'*.

"*Fumez-vous?*"

I hesitated, but as it seems that everyone in France smokes, I take my chances.

"*Oui, un peu*"

"*OK, bien*" she responds, and with that stamps the required certificate, and hands it to me.

And just like that, I passed my French medical exam.

Paperwork Victories: The Joy of the receiving your Carte de Vitale

In a county with a world-renowned reputation for the quality of its healthcare, here's your access card. These little beauties are the holy grail.

In order to get it, you need to (in exactly the right order, although this isn't published anywhere of course)

- Register with URSSAF the French social security system
- Go through the saga of proving you exist (heaven forbid the different French administration systems talk to each other)
- Obtain a RIB (certificate provided by your French bank account – so you need one of those set up too)

What ensues is the inevitable back/forth. For this application I **had to** pay to have my birth certificate formally translated and certified in French (50 euros, *merci*). They wanted my parents' marriage certificate translated too, but I held firm (Refer to chapter on '*Pas Possible*'), and begrudgingly they finally accepted.

What makes it all the more confusing/frustrating with French administration is when you get these curveballs, requests to provide information that
a) you haven't been asked for in the first place – I'm sure they make it up as they go along, and
b) has not been a requirement in any prior (more important) application, like for example, my actual residency application! Or,
c) It's so left-field – for example, your grandmothers next-door neighbours maiden name (ok I'm being flippant)

But, the struggle is real.

Then you wait… And one day your friendly *facteur* (postman) beeps in his yellow van, and your green card has arrived. I tell you, the moment you hold that little baby in your hands, you feel like you've **won an Olympic medal**. You're one step French-er.

The Four-Day Civic Training Course: A Crash Course in French-ness

If you ever find yourself applying for residency (e.g. you're emigrating and working) in France, brace yourself—because at some point, you'll likely be summoned for a four-day civic training course, designed to integrate you into French society. Sounds practical, right? Think again.

I turned up at a government building in Niort, not knowing quite what to expect. Would I be given tips on how to navigate French bureaucracy? Maybe even a step-by-step guide on how to eat cheese in the correct order?

Who knows? It was all in French.

Lost in Translation (Or Lack of One)

To be fair, they usually provide a translator but as I did ok on the earlier French test, I was deemed not to need one.

Theoretically, I was supposed to understand what was going on.

A few hours in, it **finally dawned on me**. I'd assumed, naively, that we were all in the same boat—newcomers to France, struggling with the language and bureaucracy. But nope. Everyone else was from French-speaking Africa, and French was their first language. I was the only one who was still in the process of learning French from scratch.

So while I spent four days mentally translating everything into English and trying to keep up, they were casually chatting away, asking complex questions, and probably wondering why I looked **permanently confused**.

What you're expected to cover

Over four days, we covered some very important topics to help us settle into French life:

1. **French Values of the République** – *Liberté, égalité, fraternité...* and striking at the slightest inconvenience.

2. **French History** – Which I definitely should have found interesting, but mostly, I was just focusing on keeping up.

3. **French Laws** – Such as the importance of saying bonjour to absolutely everyone, and that forced marriages and polygamy were forbidden (which caused some lively and fascinating debate from my African classmates).

4. **Practical Stuff** – Like healthcare, the social security system, and how to open a bank account without crying (except the course being delivered in month 6 after I'd already sorted all of this, rendered it largely useless).

5. **A Final Test** – To check we've been paying attention and because nothing says welcome to France like a pop quiz on *La Révolution*.

The Accidental Lunch Date

Day one, lunchtime. The guy sitting next to me casually asked what I had for lunch.

"*Rien*" (nothing) I said.

He nodded, he'd heard there was a McDonalds around the corner.

He must have seen my ears prick up at McDonalds. That was all the confirmation he needed.

Next thing I knew, I was in McDonalds, sitting opposite a guy I didn't know 3 hours ago (does this class as a date?) awkwardly eating fries, having been tricked into a lunch date simply by being too Britishly polite to say "No".

And the worst part? I'd been looking forward to a break from speaking French!

We did however, speak about the civil war in his birth country: Central African Republic. Which I'd never heard of, yet it had been going on for years—decades, even—and had forced him to leave behind everything. So very sad, and an enlightening experience for me. A lesson learnt, about being judgey-judgey, Marie!

On day two, an American girl named Kaitlynn arrived, and made a beeline for me.

She was married to a French guy, and had a surprisingly good sense of humour for an American!

Finally! An English speaker! Suddenly, I wasn't the only one occasionally looking lost. We quickly fell into a translation routine—if she didn't understand something, I'd attempt to explain it, and if I missed something, she'd fill me in. Between us, we got through.

Just before lunch, a note was passed around the group:

"*Restez ici pour déjeuner svp*" (Stay here for lunch please). Sounded… **ominous.**

Lunch for Fifteen

So instead of scattering for lunch, we all stayed put—and it transpired one of our classmates, Therese had cooked an African feast for the entire group. No small feat, there were fifteen of us!

We shared some rice, chicken, some kind of fried fish, and many things I have no idea – all verrry, verrry spicy. I ate with caution, but it was a heartwarming and unexpected gestures to experience this during a government-run integration course.

Before this, I hadn't really thought much about who else goes through this process. I'd just assumed it was other Brits navigating post-Brexit residency rules, or maybe some Europeans settling in France.

Instead, I met people who had fled civil wars, been separated from their families for years, and had come to France not for the wine and cheese, but because they had no choice.

By the end of the course, I had:

- Learned an entire history of France that I'd mostly forgotten by the next week.
- Discovered that French bureaucracy even extends to learning about French bureaucracy.
- Been humbled by the experiences of the people around me.

And, of course, I had a brand-new certificate to prove that I was officially *intégrée* into French society.

Not that the *boulangerie* lady would agree—she was still correcting my pronunciation. "***une** baguette*" (as opposed to my *un baguette*).

The Joy of Dealing with ANTS (And Not the Kind that March in a Line.)

When you hear the name ANTS (*Agence Nationale des Titres Sécurisés*), you might picture something efficient, orderly—perhaps a colony of actual ants, working together with impressive precision. **Spoiler alert: they are nothing like ants.**

Our adventure with ANTS started, as most bureaucratic nightmares do, with a simple goal: importing a car and a trailer. How hard could it be?

Turns out, very.

In search of a piece of paper – The Certificate of Conformity

This certificate is an official document proving that your vehicle meets European standards – the golden ticket to allow it to be registered in France.

Credit where credit is due, BMW were super-efficient in providing this for the car. The trailer, was too old so thankfully being an iFor Williams – I could get an 'equivalent' Barre Rouge – which is essentially a French technical approval document from the manufacturer. First up, I had to register the trailer in my name in the UK - who even knew this was a thing?

I had inherited this trailer from my dad, who (ever the bargain hunter) had sourced it second-hand off eBay 10ish years prior). The only proof of purchase being a hand scrawled note.

Initially I was passed around various iFor Williams service departments - the UK to France, then back to the UK (different branch). Luckily on the 3rd call, the lady took some pity on me (she must have heard the desperation in my voice), and agreed to update their records, and 10 days later, the Barre Rouge arrives.

Great I thought, let's start the process.

Now I'd read a few expat groups on the matter at this point. One chap seemed to have found a lucrative niche and was offering his services to do the process on your behalf – for a small fee of course!

I, however, was never one to shy away from a challenge. I mean **how hard could it be**?

Customs Paperwork was "Pas Grave"—Except It Was

You may recall at border control, I didn't get my customs form stamped at the same time as my visa.

"No worries," they'd said. *"Pas grave!"*

Let me tell you—it was indeed grave.

Fast-forward to trying to register the car and trailer, and suddenly this missing stamp was a huge problem.

It was necessary to contact the local Douanes (customs), my nearest being La Rochelle. 45 minutes away.

The first time I emailed, they told me it was impossible to fix. I'd need to pay the import tax – which I calculated online to be about 10k - nearly the value of the car.

You learn quickly that if you ask a French official whether something is possible, the default answer is generally no.

- Can I register my trailer? *Impossible.*

- Can I register my car? *Pas possible.*

But the trick of making the impossible, possible is to keep asking in slightly different ways until someone miraculously changes their mind.

By the 15th email, after rewording my request slightly, *"Ah oui, c'est possible."*

There was a catch. I'd need to go to La Rochelle with all my paperwork, and for an 'inspection'.

The dread-ed DREAL

The expat group was full of horror stories regarding these Douane inspections. They often seemed to set out stringent requirements like changing headlights to conform to French standards – hundreds, sometimes thousands of pounds worth of garage bills followed.

I made two separate trips to La Rochelle, because on one day, I was told I needed a DREAL inspection, and on another day, I was told I didn't.

Excellent use of time.

On the second trip, the customs official I'd been emailing wasn't in the office. His colleague, hearing my pleas (having originally asked me to come back a 3rd time), reluctantly agreed to do the inspection.

He examined the car from a few different angles, took a note of the VIN, and agreed we were fine. He didn't have time to do the customs paperwork now (despite him spending most of the 60 minutes I was there chatting with his colleague about nothing work related). Nope, instead he'd leave it for my previous contact to do when he was back from holiday.

After a couple of weeks and hearing nothing, I chased.

Now back from holiday, my contact would do the paperwork, but I'd need another trip to La Rochelle to collect it.

"Can you not just post it?"

"Pas Possible"

Some back and forth, and he finally agreed to send it to me in the post, provided I (by return) sent back a signed copy of a form. **Do you see the pattern here?**

Yet finally, I was ready to start the ANTS process.

The Ant Hill of Paperwork.

You never see an actual person from ANTS, because everything is online.

Once you've managed to log in, a technical feat in itself, even for someone who considers themselves pretty IT savvy.

Their "mound" is a web of paperwork. Suddenly you're knee deep in pages of personal information, and scanning documents. You believe you've supplied everything..

Yet each response reveals new demands: a missing signature, or a pixelated scan.

And just like real ants they have an uncanny ability to pop up when you're just about to relax – such as on a Sunday afternoon.

"**URGENT:** You have 24 hours to provide additional documents of your file will be cancelled".

Your Sunday evening then spent rummaging through old paperwork to dig out that 2016 electricity bill.

That trailer proof of ownership rears its head again of course.

"You need the original proof of purchase."

"That is all I have."

"Then it's *impossible*."

Until it's not.

This is the ANTS experience in a nutshell.

At this point, to be honest, I considered setting fire to the car, and just walking everywhere.

The Carte Grise

A bit like the Carte Vitale, a wave of excitement when it finally arrives in the post – you order your new French number plates, you feel even French-er as you're driving around.

Until you realise you'll now be picked up on the speed cameras. Just 1kmph over it transpires, is enough to receive a lovely fine in the post. Which we came to realise (the hard way) in that very first week.

To this day, I still don't have the carte grise for the trailer.

ANTS sent it to the wrong address.

- I contacted them to correct it.
- They required me to re-prove everything and more (despite it being their mistake).
- Now they won't send me the new carte grise until I return the original.
- The original which, reminder: I never received.

After 242 emails, I'm still building up the strength to respond.

False sense of Assurance

Now that I had the car in France legally, I needed *assurance* (insurance).

No comparison websites here – you pop into your local insurance broker in town and arrange it face to face – how novel.

First issue: They wanted a French driving licence. Except you can't get one of those until you've lived in France for 12 months.

Second issue: They needed proof of my insurance since I passed my test.

Me: "That was 20 years ago."

Them: "Oui."

Me: "In the UK, you shop around online every year, and never keep the paperwork."

Them: shrug

Third issue: They wouldn't accept my UK no-claims discount because it wasn't in French.

But remember *"Pas Possible"* is as French as baguettes and brie. And behind every *Pas Possible* lies the hidden truth: It's actually possible. **Keep asking. Reword your request. Wear them down.**

French Bureaucracy Bingo

To keep some sanity, and make light of a bad situation, I start playing bingo every time I embark on a new administration process.

YOU'RE TOLD *'C'EST PAS POSSIBLE'* WHEN IT ACTUALLY IS	YOU RECEIVE A LETTER TELLING YOU TO GO ONLINE, THEN THE WEBSITE TELLS YOU TO GO IN PERSON	YOU'VE BEEN ASKED TO SUBMIT A DOCUMENT THAT DOESN'T EXIST
YOU'VE BEEN ASKED FOR A BIRTH CERTIFICATE ISSUED IN THE LAST 3 MONTHS (AS IF SOMETHING HAS CHANGED)	YOU NEED TO GET A DOCUMENT STAMPED, BUT THE PERSON THAT NEEDS TO DO IT IS ON HOLIDAY FOR 3 WEEKS	YOUR UTILITY BILL DOESN'T COUNT AS PROOF OF ADDRESS
YOU'VE BEEN ASKED TO SUBMIT A DOSSIER WITH AT LEAST 20 SUPPORTING DOCUMENTS	YOU'VE BEEN TOLD CONTRADICTORY INFORMATION BY TWO DIFFERENT OFFICIALS ON THE SAME DAY	YOU ARRIVE AT AN APPOINTMENT TO BE TOLD YOU NEED TO BOOK ANOTHER (THE PERSON YOU NEED ISN'T IN ETC)
YOU'VE SEND 243 EMAILS AND STILL DON'T HAVE A STRAIGHT ANSWER	YOU SUBMIT EVERYTHING CORRECTLY BUT ARE OLD YOU'LL HAVE TO WAIT 6 MONTHS FOR A RESPONSE	YOU'VE CONSIDERED BRIBING PREFECTURE PERSONNEL WITH WINE

Now if you ever get **BINGO** – Congratulations – you've officially mastered French administration!

Whilst I've most definitely never done one, I would liken the process to running a marathon. Exhausting, repetitive and by the end of it you're pretty sure you don't ever want to do it again. But once scaled, anther challenge always awaits – like finding a place that feels like home.

Because apparently mastering French admin, was **just the warm up**.

Finding a Home: A Full-Time Job with a Side of Mystery

Selling or Buying a house in France isn't so much a process as it is an endurance sport. It will test your patience, your sanity, and your ability to decipher estate agent listings that seem to be written in a language all of their own.

Forget the British system of neatly categorised listings, instant Rightmove alerts, and eager estate agents practically throwing keys at you—this is France, where trying to sell or buy a house is an adventure in perseverance, detective work, and a lot of unanswered phone calls.

Do They Even Want to Sell Houses?

One of the great mysteries is whether estate agents actually want to sell you a house. You'd think that expressing an interest in a property would result in enthusiasm, follow-ups, maybe even a viewing. Not here. Instead, expect to call at least 15 times before someone reluctantly picks up, sounding vaguely surprised that you're still interested. If you send an email? Forget it.

Let's talk about fees. Oh the Fees! In the UK, you might grumble about a 1-2% estate agent fee. In France? Try 10%. And that's before you add the *notaire's* fees. That bargain countryside retreat suddenly isn't looking quite so cheap once you've factored in all the extras.

And where is Rightmove? One of the most frustrating parts of house hunting in France is that there is no single place where all the listings exist. There's no Rightmove, no Zoopla. The closest thing is Green-Acres, but a huge number of agents aren't even on there. Instead, you'll need to trawl through multiple websites, make millions of calls, and drive around looking for *à vendre* signs.

A Game of Guess the Location

French estate agents love secrecy. In the UK, you get an address and a floor plan before you even step foot in a house. Here you'll get a grainy photo of a random doorway and a vague description like 'charming village property' (which could mean anything from a crumbling ruin to a *château*). They won't give you the address upfront (as they are scared about losing that giant fee obviously), so you end up playing detective, scanning Google Maps for suspiciously familiar rooftops and driving around peering over hedges. I have got so skilled at this now, I could make a business out of tracking these places down. Honestly though, I wish they'd just tell me the bloody address—It would save us both a lot of time.

Comparing Houses? Good Luck!

In the UK, you can compare houses by number of bedrooms, location, and overall condition. In France, it's like comparing apples to accordions. One house might be a 17th-century stone farmhouse with a *pigeonnier* and ancient beams, while the next is a breeze-block rectangle with a roof. One will have a fully restored interior; the other will have a kitchen that hasn't seen an upgrade since 1973. Trying to create a shortlist is impossible because no two houses are remotely alike.

Estate agent descriptions in France range from overly poetic to painfully vague. A house listed as needs updating probably has no roof. Full of character means that 1970s bathroom is in a shade of green that hasn't been in fashion since the 70's. And potential? Well, that usually means "bring a bulldozer."

The Wild Price Variations

Two houses, same village, similar size—one is €80,000, the other is €250,000. Why? Nobody knows. Pricing in France appears to be based on vibes rather than logic. Some properties are listed at reasonable market value, while others....

The French Love Style… Just Not in Their Homes

French people are effortlessly chic—perfectly tailored coats, understated jewellery. Their homes? A wild mix of old and new that often makes no sense. Picture a stunning old stone farmhouse with original beams… and a glossy futuristic red IKEA kitchen that looks like it was beamed in from another planet. It's a design paradox, and one I'll never quite understand.

In the UK, if you build with breeze block, you render it. In France? They just leave it. Whole villages of unfinished-looking houses, as if everyone collectively decided to stop halfway through. Maybe it's a trend. Maybe it's just… France.

House Hunting Horrors

We were serious buyers. This was the day we were going to find our dream home.

We'd booked a full day with Katie, an estate agent who'd promised to show us everything she had that matched our wish list.

We'd ruled out a couple straight away having seen some details, but she'd thrown some wild cards in – because as we'd come to learn, estate agents in France don't always believe you know what you actually want.

The plan was simple: we'd meet at the first house, then follow her for the rest of the day.

We warmed to Katie straight away. She turned up a little late (only by a minute or two which isn't really late by French standards), a bit flustered, and armed with a thick folder of house details.

She handed it over, cracked a joke that had us all laughing hard, and we instantly knew this was going to be a fun day.

House #1: It has 'Potential' for needing a new roof

It needed a bit of TLC she warned as she was trying to kick down the door through the over grown ivy. It had no kitchen, no bathroom, and only half a roof.

As we continued walking around it got worse. No double glazing, no septic tank.

I mean it was basically a barn.

We had said we would consider a project… but building a whole house may be a stretch.

OK. Next.

House #2: The Paedo House

Set deep into the countryside, we pulled up outside a pretty ordinary looking house. It wasn't love at first sight, but we weren't here to judge a book by its cover.

We stepped inside. It felt eerily cold. The layout was very odd, and it just got weirder as we made our way upstairs.

The upstairs had been divided into lots of small bedrooms, each with either a very small or blocked up window, and a **lock on the door**. Each bedroom was distinctly different. Whether covered in posters of 80's pop stars, or another which was typically boy-themed, blue and adorned with sports cars. Weird creepy dolls in the third, and a medical poster of someone breastfeeding?!

It was all **very odd**.

"Err, any ideas on the previous owner" I asked.

Katie hesitated.

"I think he may have fostered some children" she said.

Not reassuring.

"Maybe let's move onto the next one" I said quickly, backing towards the door.

House #3: Gangsters paradise

After shaking off the unsettling energy of the last house, we followed Katie onwards.

"Now this is owned by a man from the South" she said, as if that explained something.

She knocked at the door. The door swung open almost instantly.

A man stood there, wearing half an unbuttoned shirt, a thick gold chain, and a tan that suggested he hadn't done an honest days' work in decades. He looked us up and down, muttered something at Katie and walked inside.

We glanced at Katie.

"He's from Nice", she whispered. "Very South of France".

The house inside was immaculate. Marble floors, and very light cream, almost white furniture. It didn't look remotely lived in.

The upstairs had potential for conversion, Katie explained.

When we entered the loft space, we were greeted with a human punch bag, loads of other military equipment (as if the owner had raided an army surplus). And handcuffs…

We took that as our cue to wrap things up, and headed back downstairs. Heading out the back door into the garden, we heard barking and froze.

Another bark. Louder. Closer.

Then from the depths of the overgrown garden, a huge Alsation appeared.

"RUN!" shrieked Katie, using me as a human shield to save herself.

We ran like our lives depended on it, only to see the dog hurl itself at some fence we didn't know existed. **Thank god for that fence.** Now that we knew we weren't going to be eaten alive, we laughed. A lot.

Despite the madness, the endless calls, and the detective work, you will eventually find your dream French home. It might come with an ancient septic tank, a mysterious outbuilding full of wildlife, and questionable interior choices—but it will be yours. And once you're sitting outside on your terrace, looking at your very own slice of France, it will all feel worth it.

...Until the next round of paperwork arrives of course.

Living in a Stone Charentaise Longère: Picturesque or Punishment?

Ah, the *Charentaise longère*—the quintessential French dream home. A long one-storey rectangular house built of local stone, orientated so the back is to the prevailing winds. Exposed beams, creamy thick stone walls, wooden shutters... the kind of place you see in glossy property magazines with words like *"charmant"* and *"authentique"* thrown around.

And yes, it is stunning. In summer, the birds are singing and the sun shines over the fields of sunflowers and rolling hills with grapevines.

Not exaggerating. The view from our house is so pretty that Van Gogh and Monet could come to blows over it. The *longère* provides cool, natural air-conditioning, when it's melting outside.

But then comes winter.

And suddenly, your beautiful French dream home turns into a medieval survival challenge.

If you've never lived in a 200-year-old stone house with no insulation, let me also explain the heating situation: there isn't any.

Okay, fine, but not by traditional standards. We have 2 wood burners—a big, iron one in the kitchen, and a smaller one in the lounge.

They demand constant 'feeding' so I feel like I spend half of my life in the winter, hauling logs and muttering under my breath about "living in the dark ages"'

Meanwhile, the stone walls do an excellent job of trapping the cold inside. No matter what temperature it is outdoors, inside remains at a steady mildly refrigerated state—perfect for storing cheese, less ideal for human survival.

Three Months of Winter Misery

Never have I experienced cold like this.

- Waking up to see our own breath.. indoors.
- A level of mental preparation required just to get out of bed.
- If we hadn't owned an electric blanket, I tell you we'd be writing this from beyond the grave.

Wearing four layers and a coat inside is the norm. Dressing for bed means putting on thermal socks, a hoodie, and possibly a hat. And heaven forbid you've forgotten to put the electric blanket on an hour before to get warmed up.

I'll be on facetime to a friend back home and they'll say something like:

"Ooh, I bet it's so much warmer in France this time of year!".

I stare at them in disbelief, resenting them, and their insulated new builds with central heating. Meanwhile I'm casing the joint for anything I can burn to make it through the night.

Belle who is not used to living in these kind of arctic conditions, just stares at me shivering and looking continually miffed.

The Weird 'Between Seasons' Problem"

Then like a flash, spring arrives. The sun starts shining, the countryside bursts into life, and you foolishly think, It's over! I've survived!

Nope. You have entered the limbo zone.

For the next two months, it will be warmer outside than inside. You'll step outside into a lovely, mild spring day, then walk back inside and immediately need a jumper. The *longère* remains cold, completely impervious to the season. I often wonder if I'd be better off sleeping outside for some warmth.

Then comes summer. And the house is magical. It stays cool and refreshing while the outside world bakes in the 40+ degree Charente-Maritime heat. As you step outside, you feel the 'rush' like when you get off an aeroplane somewhere hot.

You smugly retreat indoors during the afternoon when it gets too much, congratulating yourself on making such a wise property decision.

Then you go upstairs to bed.

And realise that your *longère* has a dark secret.

Because while the downstairs remains a cool paradise, the upstairs—thanks to the zero insulation and a roof designed to trap heat like an oven—becomes a literal hot box.

It doesn't matter how many fans you have, air just doesn't move. You try to sleep, sweating like you've just run a marathon, wondering if the people who lived here in the 1800s just accepted slow-cooking themselves to death. One fretful night of "I can't cope with this, Tom" for the 673rd time that night, you cave. Queue Amazon delivery of an air-con unit for tomorrow – France has Prime too, you know!

Yet despite everything—the winter suffering, the temperature whiplash, the log-hauling lifestyle—I wouldn't swap it. Not yet, anyway.

Because for six glorious months of the year, a stone *longère* is the perfect home. Cool (downstairs at least) in the summer, charming in spring/autumn, and the ideal backdrop for *apéro-fuelled* evenings under the stars.

And for the other six months? Well… there's always the electric blanket and air con.

Everyday Life: Learning the French Way

Saying Bonjour to Everything That Moves

Nobody tells you this before you move to France, but you *bonjour* **everything**.

- Enter the *boulangerie*, *"bonjour"*
- Walk past someone in the street, *"bonjour"*
- When you arrive at a restaurant, or when a new waiter serves you, *"bonjour"*
- Basically before **any** interaction, *"bonjour"*

It's the social currency – the way to get anything done.

The unwritten rule: no bonjour = no service

You enter a boulangerie *"Une baguette, s'il vous plaît."*. They'll stare right through you, even if you repeat your order. "Euh… *une baguette?"*

Silence.

You rack your brains whether you've gendered baguette properly. Yep, it's definitely feminine. Finally, some old man behind you in the queue may help you out by whispering *"Vous n'avez pas dit bonjour."* (you haven't said bonjour)

Penny drops. You turn around and croak *"bonjour"*. Instantly the *boulanger* smiles warmly and comes to life. *"Ahhh, bonjour! Une baguette? Voilà, madame! Bonne journée!"*

You come to realise, you could be collapsed on the floor having a heart attack, and whoever comes to your assistance would probably still expect you to say bonjour first!

The difference between bonjour and bonsoir – the tricky changeover

This linguistic tripwire is designed to expose foreigners at every opportunity.

In France you see, there is a deeply ingrained, but completely unwritten rule; at some point in the late afternoon *bonjour* (hello) suddenly becomes *bonsoir* (good evening).

If you get it wrong, instant regret, and silent judging by your French counterpart.

So when exactly does it change? Good question.

One might assume sun set? Nope.

The general rule is 6pm, except when it's not. Some start saying bonsoir at 5.30pm, some wait until 7pm. Others seem to switch whenever they feel like it just to confuse (or humiliate) you.

I asked my French teacher once, who stared at me blankly *"c'est evident"* was the reply.. Hmmm, no actually it's not.

It's like an invisible social contract that everyone in France instinctively understands – except you.

- **Say Bonjour too late** (absolute *faux pas*) – you'll be met with a look of deep disappointment, and a church bell will ring ominously in the distance
- **Overcorrect too early** (The over enthusiastic *Bonsoir*) – it might be 4.45pm, sun is still up, but you panic. You're greeted with a smirk. How adorable, the little foreigner thinks it's evening already. They will of course respond with *bonjour* – a subtle, yet devastating correction to confirm you have failed the test.

- **Hesitate mid greeting** (even a quick side glance at your phone home screen) – You mumble *bon-jo-soir*. A raised eyebrow tells you the damage is done.

Survival strategies: Mumble something starting with 'bon', at least confidently, and flash a big smile

Back to the Future(book)

At the time I moved to France, I had spent years smugly off Facebook. I'd escaped. No more endless baby updates, school friends selling things you don't need, holiday pics that make you seethe with jealousy when you're working, or someone's dinner photographed at four angles. My life was gloriously offline. Unreachable. Free.

Then we moved to rural France.

Where it's 2025, but also… somehow still 2009.

Suddenly, everyone — and everything — is on Facebook. Not ironically. Not just for Marketplace or stalking exes. Genuinely on it. Actively.

Posting things like "Lost Dog" or "*Vide grenier* this Sunday."

No posters, no websites. Just… Facebook.

Want to know what time the mobile pizza van turns up? Facebook.

Which day the local pool is actually open despite the sign saying "*Ouvert*"? Facebook.

Is there a *brocante* happening in a field somewhere? Facebook.

I reactivated my old account with a sense of quiet shame.

My profile picture was still from a holiday in 2017. I blinked into the blue light, added myself to "*Les Amis de Saint Jean*" and "*Actualités de Surgeres et alentours*", and was instantly flooded with information I didn't even know I needed.

Turns out you can take the Brit out of Facebook, but move to rural France and Facebook will absolutely take you back.

The Best Healthcare You Can't Actually Access

As we know, France is renowned for having one of the best healthcare systems in the world—efficient, affordable, and packed with highly skilled doctors. In theory, it's a dream. In practice? Well, good luck actually registering with a doctor or dentist.

You'd think moving to rural France would mean an abundance of friendly GPs just waiting to take on new patients. Instead, it's a game of medical musical chairs—except all the chairs were taken years ago, and **no one's moving**.

You call up a *médecin généraliste*, only to be met with a weary "*Désolé, nous ne prenons plus de nouveaux patients.*" ("Sorry, we're not taking new patients.") Try another? Same story. At this point, you'd have better luck getting an audience with the Pope.

Then there's the dentist situation. Teeth rotting? Filling fallen out? Desperate for a check-up? *Tant pis!* The nearest available appointment is in six months—if you're lucky.

And then there's Doctolib, France's online booking system that's meant to make getting medical appointments easier.

Instead, it becomes a **daily exercise in disappointment**. You optimistically search for a doctor nearby. No results. You widen the search radius. Still nothing. You start clicking on any doctor within a 100km radius, just in case. You finally see an opening—but it's for a dermatologist in December.

So while the French healthcare system is excellent if you're in it, actually getting into it is another matter entirely. They say patience is a virtue, but when it comes to finding a *médecin*, it's more of a survival skill.

Friday Night Dining Phenomenon: Arrive early or starve

The week is done, and suddenly the streets hum with that unmistakeable Friday Feeling.

You'll often find us in the square, where the restaurant tables spill into the street. An ancient fountain in the corner, the towers of the Abbey peeking over the buildings.

There's a buzz in the air. Relaxed conversation, locals greeting with the double *bise*.

After a leisurely drink (or several), we're thinking about dinner.

If you haven't booked ahead and you're trying to sit down at 8pm, **good luck**. The French descend en masse at precisely that moment.

It's a sure-fire way to spot the Brits. Eating almost alone in the restaurant at 7pm, looking pleased with themselves for getting a table.

The French sometimes strolling in fashionably late – sauntering into the restaurant at 10.30pm? It gives me indigestion just thinking about it.

French families are out in force, kids still awake at 11pm, sitting to the table eating something really *'adulte'* like a *tartare de boeuf*. No chicken nuggets available here I'm afraid.

Or you'll watch them playing quietly off to the side of the street. Always makes you question why British children are herded to bed so early.

Eating out is one of our favourite hobbies – provided we book ahead to eat at British O'clock that is.

You quickly learn, you need to give yourself time. Dinner here is a marathon, not a sprint. So if you're hoping to be tucked up in bed by 10pm, you're in the wrong country.

Scat Man & Moules Frites – Jazz Nights at Café Boulevard

Tucked away in a little corner of a town nearby, Café Boulevard is one of those places that feels like it hasn't changed in years—and doesn't intend to anytime soon.

A small, unassuming spot where on the first Friday of each month for 12 euros, you get a three-course meal and a live jazz band.

The night starts strong. A proper jazz band— piano, double bass, sax, the works—playing away while the small crowd sips their wine and nods appreciatively.

But then, just as you're really getting into it, the music stops. Not for a dramatic pause, not for a slow interlude—no, it stops because dinner is ready. The band members put down their instruments, pull up chairs on the table right next to you, and tuck into their moules frites like it's the most normal thing in the world. Because, in France, it is.

After dinner comes the improvisation session. This is where things get interesting. Enter Scat Man: an elderly gentleman, possibly in his late eighties (hard to tell), who takes to the stage with the energy of a man possessed. He grips the microphone, eyes closed, one hand raised to the heavens like he's summoning the spirit of jazz itself. And then—he **lets loose**.

"Skib-ee-dab-skib-op-bwooo-dap!"

The room holds its breath.

"Bzzt-zop-dee-wah-dibby-dibby-doo!"

Wine glasses tremble.

"Bop! Bop! Shoo-wop-de-wop-zip-ZEEEEE!"

The man is shaking. The jazz is flowing through him. He is unstoppable.

The crowd? Loving it. The atmosphere? Impeccable. The wine? Flowing.

Among the mostly French audience, there are a few expats who show up every time. One old chap, in particular, has taken a liking to Tom. Every time we go, without fail, he greets Tom with a hearty, "Ah, young man!" before launching into a conversation about food. For some unknown reason, he's convinced that Tom used to be a chef in the military. He was not. He has never been. But the old boy is so enthusiastic about it, Tom just nods along now. "So, what have you been cooking up lately?" he'll ask, and Tom, who at best has reheated last night's leftovers, will scramble to think of something **suitably cheffy**.

By the end of the night, we always leave a little tipsy, a little deaf from the scat session, and very full from what is probably the best-value meal in town. And we know, next time, the old chap will be waiting to ask Tom about his latest culinary masterpiece.

Locked in & Liquored up with the Locals

Outside of the town, our closest bar is in the next village. An unassuming place, a mix of old and new décor, including a back wall of undecorated plasterboard. It does however have a real log fire – very novel for a bar in France.

The first time we stumbled in, we were met with the kind of stares usually reserved for Wild West saloons. Every head turned. Every conversation paused. All eyes on us.

"Bonsoir!" we announced nervously, shuffling toward the bar.

A warm chorus of *"Bonsoir!"* followed, along with a sea of smiles—then everyone casually turned back to their conversations.

Politeness, the French way. You look someone in the eye, you greet them. Revolutionary. Still, **we'd passed the first test.**

That first night, an enthusiastic local man performed what can only be described as a strip-tease meets interpretive lap dance for Tom. His long-suffering wife? Propped up at the bar, chatting like it was just another Friday.

Same characters, every week. Two grown men asleep rather precariously balanced on bar stools, faces on the bar, not even a stir when the bar bell was being rung inches from their heads.

It's easy to see why people keep coming back. The owner memorised our drinks on night one, and before we'd even finished, he was there with the next round. All night long. Better service than most restaurants I've been to.

Closing time? Doesn't exist. They just lock the doors, put the ashtrays out on the table, and carry on. If you're in, you're in.

These days, we walk in to a warm "Bonsoir!" from the locals and a *faire la bise* from the owner.

We've played pool (badly), danced (questionably), and sung karaoke (terribly). Our French gets more fluent with each drink—or so we think.

Do we feel like locals? Not quite. But we've always felt welcome. **Never underestimate the social value of being brave enough to say *Bonsoir*.**

Weekends Spent Exploring

Why Does Everything Feel More Charming in France?

There's something about wandering through old French towns that feels a little bit... cinematic. You're never **just walking**; you're strolling (*flâner*), preferably with a croissant or baguette in hand.

The light hits the creamy-coloured stone buildings just right, there's probably a cat lazily stretching in the sun on a balconette, and somehow, every town square looks like it belongs on a postcard.

It doesn't matter how many medieval villages you visit, the magic never fades.

- **Pristine communes**, no matter how tiny, look like they have just been pressure-washed for a photoshoot.
- **The mairie** (town hall) is always immaculate, usually decorated with perfectly manicured flower boxes.
- Someone, somewhere, is **always sweeping**.

Whether it's a grand château, a simple village house with shutters, or a half-crumbled medieval ruin, everything **looks effortlessly beautiful**. No one has ever looked at a building in France and thought, "Now that could use some UPVC windows".

You Must Poke Your Head into L'Église

We always find ourselves gravitating towards the church for a nose. Even if you're not religious, you must step inside and have a look as every church is so different:

- Some are strikingly plain, just stone walls and wooden pews, exuding a quiet simplicity.

- Others are ornate masterpieces, with elaborate carvings, statues, or murals that make you stop in your tracks.

- And sometimes, you'll push open the heavy wooden door and be greeted by unexpected delights…

Lozay: The Most Perfectly Theatrical Church Experience

Just ten minutes from home, a small commune called Lozay has a lovely little unassuming church tucked away that really delivers.

You approach via a tree-lined path (which, let's be honest, already makes it a winner—who can resist a tree-lined approach?). You open the door, expecting the usual peaceful silence, and instead:

- Soft choral music begins to play through hidden speakers.

- Automatic lights gently illuminate the interior as you step inside.

- You walk down the steps, momentarily convinced you've just entered Narnia.

And yet, there is never anyone around. It's as if these little churches exist in their own pocket of time, waiting patiently for the occasional visitor to wander in, and then disappear again.

The French Weekend Ritual

A weekend spent exploring is never wasted in France. We often set off with no real plan (for anyone that knows me and my love of a plan, this is quite a feat).

We stop for a poke around a village or two. There's always something beautiful to see – an old washhouse, or roman baths. We grab some lunch, and before we know it, the whole day has disappeared in a haze of stone buildings and cobbled streets.

And somehow, given all that history, it **never gets old**.

Escaping to the Coast: The Côte Sauvage & the Islands

J'adore the coast. It was a key reason for choosing to settle here in the Charente Maritime.

Not far from the mainland, Île d'Oléron and Île de Ré offer a wonderful coastal escape for us. Both islands are connected by bridges, but are so so different.

- Île d'Oléron is bigger, wilder, and more rugged, perfect exploring hidden beaches, fishing ports, and the famous colourful oyster huts. The fresh seafood is **incredible..**

- Île de Ré is the chic, picture-perfect island—think whitewashed villages, cobbled streets, and bikes with little baskets to carry your *baguette* back from the *boulanger*. It's very elegant, and very French.

But our favourite place to go, probably bolstered by fond childhood memories, is the *Côte Sauvage* (literally Wild Coast). Which unlike the usual built-up coastal tourist trap delivers miles of golden sandy beaches, dramatic dunes, and barely another soul in sight. It's **untouched**.

When you arrive, you're first met with the strong scent of pine needles filling the air. The forest seems to stretch on forever, broken only by cycle tracks and hidden sandy paths leading to the ocean.

Then, suddenly, the trees part, and there it is: the Atlantic in all its wild glory. No high-rise hotels, no ugly concrete promenades, just rolling dunes, golden sand, and the sound of waves crashing on the shore. Out of season, you can have an entire stretch of beach (for miles) **all to yourselves**. The dogs are in paradise.

It's like a best-kept secret. So shhhh, don't tell anyone.

We day trip to the coast often, and even take the camper for extended trips to the islands whenever we get the chance (a.k.a. it's not broken down).

There's something about feeling soft sand between your toes which is good for the soul – although I'd suggest you skip going barefoot as you make the long and arduous trek back over the dunes - unless you enjoy getting spiked between the toes by pine needles that is.

Sinking feeling - a relaxing swim in Fouras

It was one of those scorching summer days. Riding to the beach on the motorbike was less "refreshing sea air" and more like "being blasted by a giant hairdryer on full heat." But we had a plan—cool off with a swim, float about in the sea, maybe even have an ice cream and a drink afterwards. Idyllic.

Fouras is our closest beach, and while it's no Côte d'Azur, it does the job. It has a sandy beach, and whilst sitting there your view consists of the Fort to one side, and the islands on the horizon on a clear day.

We spotted a pontoon floating out in the water and thought, let's swim out to it. So off we went, eager for a **refreshing dip.**

The first clue that something was off? The texture underfoot as we entered the water. It wasn't the pleasant, grainy feeling of soft sand—it was squelchy. **Suspiciously squelchy**. Each step felt like we were sinking ever so slightly, but we pushed on, determined.

We made it to the pontoon, feeling triumphant. The sun was shining, the water was cool, and we basked in the sunshine for a while. And then… we noticed something troubling.

The tide. It was going out. Fast. Fouras you see, is situated on the mouth of the Charente estuary.

Back into the water we went, but now, instead of wading through the shallows, we were sinking. Deep. My foot disappeared into the mud. Then my ankle. Then my thigh. This was no longer a swim; this was quicksand survival training. Tom was, of course, in his **element.**

I looked over to see another woman, tears streaming down her face, desperately clinging to her boyfriend. Meanwhile, the lifeguards? Just standing on the shore, watching. No sense of urgency. No attempt to help. Just the classic French shrug, as if to say, Well, you chose to swim there, didn't you?

After what felt like an eternity of wading, yanking, and desperately trying not to panic, we finally made it back to shore. The romantic idea of a refreshing seaside dip had turned into an unexpected full-body mud bath. An embarrassing walk up the beach ensued, head to toe in brown sludge, **questioning all of our life choices.**

I'd suggest if you ever find yourself in Fouras and fancy a dip - check the tide times—or bring a shovel.

Closed Until Further Notice (or Whenever They Feel Like It)

You should be prepared that winter in France is a quiet affair. And by "quiet," I mean **everything closes.**

The *boulangerie?* Gone fishing.

The little café where you like to sit and watch the world go by? *Fermé jusqu'au printemps.*

You may as well reside to bunkering down with Netflix and hibernating until April.

But even outside of winter, France operates on a schedule that can only be described as **deeply relaxed**.

- Sundays? Closed.
- Monday mornings? Closed.
- Random weekday afternoons? Also closed.

Feel like a late lunch at 2:01 PM? Tough luck. Should have planned better.

Then there's the true enigma: *fermeture exceptionnelle*. A phrase that roughly translates to, "We have closed for absolutely no reason, and we do not owe you an explanation." It could be anything—staff holidays, a power cut, or maybe they just couldn't be bothered that day. Who knows? Not you. Not anyone.

One of my favourite experiences of French business hours happened in the Dordogne. We were staying in a little town where the only bar in the square was buzzing—people drinking, laughing, enjoying the summer evening. And then, suddenly, the staff started stacking chairs.

"Closing time already?" we asked, confused.

"Oh no," the bartender replied cheerfully. "We're shutting for the next two weeks. The owner is on holiday!"

That's right. The only bar, in the middle of peak tourist season, was closing so the owner could go and enjoy himself. Imagine a British pub landlord doing that. You'd have a full-scale revolt. But here? Nobody blinked. Just nodded, sipped their wine, and presumably planned to return in three weeks.

August it transpires, isn't just a month in France – it's a mass exodus. Shops, bakeries, even entire businesses shut down as the French head off on holiday

So, if you're thinking of moving to France, take up a hobby. A good one. Anything to keep you occupied during the winter downtime and the long stretches of unexplained closure. Maybe learn an instrument? Get good enough and who knows, you could find yourself in the Boulevard improvisation sesh.

Culinary Misadventures

A Fishy Proposition

Toms mum is renowned for her exceptional culinary skills. During a stay with them, and eager to express gratitude, I volunteered to prepare dinner one evening. I decided on a comforting classic fish pie – a dish I was confident in, having cooked many times, and I knew his mum loved fish. What could be better?

I ventured to the local *supermarché,* navigating the aisles with the confidence of a seasoned chef. Near the fish counter, a particular white fillet of fish caught my eye – labelled in French of course, but resembling cod. I recognised *morue,* so added it triumphantly to my basket.

Back in the kitchen, I began by poaching the fish. Noticing the filets had an unusually firm texture, and were a bit crusty. I dismissed it as a local quirk.

The sauce thickened to perfection. I indulged in a taste test. Expecting delicious creamy fishy flavours, I was hit with an avalanche of saltiness that would rival the Dead Sea.

Shit. Panic set in. I frantically added a bit more cream, then more butter, even more pepper.

I wondered if when the potatoes were on it would take the edge off. I was kidding myself.

Admitting defeat, I called into Toms mum – who was happily enjoying a wine in the living room.

"Umm Chris, would you be able to come and help me a sec".

She took one taste. Even as polite as she is, declared it totally inedible. Beyond salvage. Good for the bin.

We re-traced my steps, perplexed.

I hadn't even added any salt, had I?

Until we identified the culprit: **salted cod**. A delicacy requiring 48 hours of soaking and several water changes to remove the excess salt.

Cue a swift return to the supermarket for something else.

This lesson serving as a funny reminder of the importance of understanding local ingredients and culinary customs. Cooking in a foreign kitchen is much like navigating uncharted waters – always wise to consult a map (or in this case, an experienced local chef) before setting sail.

All that Cheese can send you crackers

France has hundreds, if not thousands of cheeses.

You'll find them in every shape and style. Tiny goats cheeses decorated in flowers, soft oozing wedges of *vieux pané*, to giant wheels of nutty *Comté*.

You can buy cheese everywhere. And the French will eat cheese either informally as a course (think nice cheeseboard), or informally (a straight up wedge of cheese).

But what happens when you want to eat it, like you would back home? With a proper cracker?

Prepare to be disappointed.

To accompany your cheese you will find biscuits that look suspiciously like sweet cookies, and crumble into dust when you try to spread your cheese onto it.

I spent hours, scanning the shelves for something that vaguely resembled a Jacobs, or a Carrs Table Water biscuit before giving up.

The French would say. "*Sacrilège*! Why do you need crackers when you can have bread?" And to be fair, **the bread here is spectacular**.

But sometimes you just want that crisp neutral crunch that only a UK cracker can provide.

A few of the hypermarkets now do stock crackers in their '*cuisine du monde*' section where you can grab a pack (if there's any left that haven't already been swiped that is) alongside your Yorkshire tea or mincemeat.

I've heard some expats have resorted to **smuggling them in** across the Channel – packing an extra suitcase full of

Jacobs. A memorable altercation if you ever got busted at customs I suppose.

I saw on a Facebook group the other day, someone had attempted to bake them herself. (far too much effort if you ask me).

I think the honest answer here, is to give up on crackers, and learn to love cheese with bread. Or just knock it back straight. After all, you're in France now, and that's apparently how it's done.

The Great Croissant Quest

If you move to France, people assume certain things: that you'll start wearing a *beret* (unironically), and that you'll have an endless supply of perfect *croissants* at your fingertips.

The reality? Not all *croissants* are created equal.

Shortly after moving here, I set out on a noble mission—to find **the one**. The perfect *croissant*. One with a golden, crisp exterior that shattered into a million buttery flakes at first bite, but with an inside that was soft, chewy, and just the right amount of moist. Not too dry, not too doughy. A delicate balance between airiness and substance.

Of course, this involved eating a lot of *croissants*. *Quel dommage!*

Some were pretty decent. Others were *pas terrible*. Either a bit too greasy. Too bready. Too much like something that had come out of a supermarket packet, rather than a *boulangerie*. The disappointment of biting into a subpar *croissant* is something I wouldn't wish on my **worst enemy**.

I learnt that not all *boulangeries* are equal either. Some are masters of *croissant* production whereas others seem to focus all their energy on *pain de campagne* and treat *croissants* as an afterthought.

Eventually, I found the one. A small bakery tucked away down a little street in our town. The first bite was everything I'd been searching for. Flaky enough to leave a small mountain of crumbs on my lap, yet soft and buttery inside. Rich but not overwhelming. A *croissant* soo good I considered immediately going back in for another.

Not every *boulangerie* deserves your loyalty. But when you find the one, you guard that secret **with your life**.

Oysters and Wine: The Simple Joys

There are few things in life as utterly blissful—and absurdly simple—as sitting in the sun, a glass of wine in hand, while nibbling on a dozen fresh *huitres*.

Now this probably sounds more glamorous than it is! If you've ever visited one of these oyster shacks, you'll know what I mean.

These little rustic shacks are proper, no-nonsense working farms, complete with weathered wood, the distinct smell of saltwater, and a pile of old oyster shells and a net shoved in the corner. Where a dozen freshest of the fresh oysters, and a couple glasses of wine will set you back the measly price of **8 euros!**

8 euros, can you believe it?!

So there you are, sitting on a simple wooden bench or a beach chair that's seen better days, the owners (and farmers) close by will happily chat with you about their oysters, explaining the different sizes (small and delicate vs big meatier ones), the subtle flavour differences, and why they're the best in the world. Wasted really, considering we always opt for a No.3's!

Shortly after your order is placed – *voilà*—your plate of oysters arrive, resting like little jewels on a bed of crushed ice. No frills, no fuss.

Served simply with a slice of lemon or maybe a little bottle of cognac vinegar (if you're feeling really fancy), and here's the twist—a crunchy baguette, **with butter!** - A huge novelty in France.

As you eat, you'll start to understand the French concept of *'profiter'* which is my favourite verb.

Which kind of broadly translates in English to 'enjoy', but it really means seizing the opportunity.

It's not just about "enjoying" the oysters; it's about savouring life's simplest pleasures, without guilt or the pressure to "do" anything more than just be present in the moment. You're doing what the French do best: **making the most out of life**.

And let's not forget the wine. It's not some Bordeaux Grand Cru —it's local white or rosé, chilled, and refreshingly perfect with the oysters.

You may wince or shudder a bit as the first gulp goes down, but the French would merely describe it as *'du caractère'*!.

And you'd certainly look a bit odd swirling it round your glass and burying your nose in it, like some kind of sommelier. That being said, it's usually, ice cold and is as unpretentious as the place itself. So you might as well order a second glass, because, well, who's counting?

And when the last oyster is gone, the last sip of wine drained, you'll look around, with a contented sigh, that you've just experienced something truly French: the perfect mix of good food, good drink, and the good life. Profiter is not just a verb here; it's a way of life. And as you head off, slightly tipsy and satisfied, you can't help but think: I'll be back next week. After all, it's only 8 euros.

My (Very Unofficial) Guide to French Wine

Before moving to France, I'd been wine tasting a handful of times. Could bluff my way through pretending to understand *tannins*, and the *terroir*.

Since living here, I'd say it's almost rude not to get involved. So here's my very unscientific guide to some of my favourites (after some dedicated research of course).

Bordeaux – The Fancy one. You have to pretend you understand all those tasting notes when drinking it. Best enjoyed while discussing the chateau you don't own.

Burgundy (Bourgougne) – The wine snobs choice. Home of the Pinot Noir which is light, elegant, and painfully expensive. We learned on our trip to Burgundy that the vineyards are divided into thousands of tiny plots – so you can have dozens of different winemakers producing their own unique wine from the same land – which is why a bottle can set you back between 5€ or 5,000€!

Loire Valley – Home to Sauvignon Blancs and Sancerre. Perfect if you want something classy, but don't want to remortgage your house for it.

Provence – *Rosé* kingdom. Light, dry and best consumed while wearing sunglasses and pretending you have a yacht.

Rhone Valley – Home to Châteauneuf-du-Pape, and other full-bodied reds that taste like they've been aged in a leather armchair. Sommeliers tip here - opt for a Lirac – same taste, fraction of the price.

Important thing about all this, is that wine in France is cheaper than water. A solid bottle of *vin de table* (a gamble which sometimes pays off) will set you back about 3€, and spending more than 5€ is considered splashing out.

So my advice, if in doubt, why not **try them all**.

Supermarket vs. Pharmacy vs. Tabac: Why Can't I Just Get Everything in One Place?

If you're used to UK supermarkets—where you can pick up a pint of milk, paracetamol, a birthday card, a garden hose, and a rotisserie chicken in one go—shopping in France might be a bit of a shock. Because in France, everything has its place. And woe betide the person who tries to buy painkillers with their groceries.

A Land of Hypermarkets and Empty Aisles

French supermarkets (or, if you're feeling brave, hypermarkets) are huge. We're talking airplane hangar levels of space. They sell everything from fresh fish to lawnmowers, and go in on a lunchtime, they always feel eerily empty—like everyone knows something you don't. If you do see someone, they are never in a rush.

Before living here, I'd happily spend hours just wandering around looking at all the different things. There are some things you can always expect from a *supermarché*:

- **A fresh food paradise** – If you love fresh produce, French supermarkets are a dream. The fruit and veg look to as if they are straight out of a food magazine, and the cheese aisle alone could be classified as a national monument.
- **Very little processed food** – If you're after a ready meal or a microwave lasagne, good luck. The French expect you to cook properly.
- **Painfully strict opening hours** – You think you'll just pop in on a Sunday afternoon? Hahaha. No. Most close at 12:30 PM on a Sunday, if they are open at all.

During the week it's 9am – 7.30pm. Working full-time, this took a little getting used to (given I used to live around the corner from a 24hr Tesco!)
- **Wine, wine, and more wine** – Entire aisles dedicated to the stuff.

You can **forget dashing in for something in a rush**. You'll walk 1.5 miles to get said item. You arrive at the *caisse*, and there could be a queue 5-deep where those in front would be obliviously having a chat to the cashier for 10 minutes about absolutely anything. And never be that person that forgot to weigh their veg.

The Pharmacy: The Only Place to Get Medicine (and a Lecture)

Need some paracetamol? You won't find it in the supermarket. Oh no, far too convenient, you need to go to a *pharmacie*.

But while French pharmacies can sometimes feel like a medical interrogation, they also offer actual advice. Try getting that level of care in Tesco.

The Tabac: A Mystery to Foreigners

Then, there's the *tabac*—a small, dimly lit shop or strange bar that somehow sells lottery tickets, cigarettes, maybe some newspapers and stamps, and occasionally, espresso.

Nobody really understands how a tabac chooses its stock, but it's a vital part of French life.

My local tabac has a cat that lives in it. Sounds endearing doesn't it – it's not. It smells really bad.

Why Is Everything So Separate?

Unlike in the UK, where supermarkets try to do everything, France believes in specialisation. Your groceries come from the supermarket. Your medicine comes from a pharmacy. If you want a pouch of tobacco, you go to the tabac.

And, yes, it's incredibly annoying when you just want to buy ibuprofen and a baguette in one trip. But it's also one of the many quirks of living in France.

You just have to plan ahead—luckily one of my favourites past times – or risk a Sunday afternoon headache with no chance of relief.

DIY Haircuts & My First French Salon Experience

For the first ten months of living in France, I cut my own hair. Not because I was particularly skilled at it—far from it in fact. More due to lack of time (too busy compiling paperwork) and because the thought of navigating a French hairdresser appointment was **frankly terrifying**. What if I accidentally asked for a mullet?

Eventually, the inevitable split ends forced me to bite the bullet. I googled how to say "Just a trim, please" and "just the split ends" at least fifteen times before booking an appointment. Armed with my well-rehearsed phrases, I stepped into the salon.

The hairdresser, a young friendly chap with a stylish crop (obviously), was horrified.

"*Vous avez coupé vos cheveux… vous-même?*" he asked, looking at me like I'd confessed to performing my own dental work.

"*Er… oui?*" I admitted.

This was apparently unacceptable. "*Mais pourquoi?*" he kept asking, over and over, as if I'd had no choice but to survive in the wilderness with only a blunt pair of kitchen scissors.

No answer seemed to satisfy him. Eventually, I just went with "*Je ne sais pas*" and **accepted my fate**.

The cut itself turned out to be more than just a haircut—it was a full-on French lesson. He even gently corrected my pronunciation as we discussed why we'd moved to France, upcoming holidays, the weather – you know, the usual hairdresser patter. Every snip came with a new piece of vocabulary. I learned how to say "blow-dry" and "grey roots" —none of which I'd ever needed before, but now seemed critical.

In the end, I walked out with perfectly trimmed hair, a confidence boost, and about twenty new 'hairdressing' words that I'd immediately forget the moment I needed them.

I learnt that sometimes, facing your fears leads to a great haircut. Sometimes, it leads to an unexpected French lesson. Either way, it's better than hacking at your own hair in the bathroom.

Popping into the local SPA & coming home with Louis

"Let's just pop in, take a look, and have a chat" Tom said. "See what the process would be"

We'd been talking about getting a second dog, a play friend for Belle. Because having two is pretty much the same as having one right? Wrong.

We'd discussed a checklist

- Small to medium sized (so we could all fit **comfortably** in the camper)
- Short-haired (as I don't want to spend all of my free time hoovering)
- Good with other dogs / kids etc (because France is super dog friendly, and I'm quite fond of my nephews & nieces pretty faces)
- Doesn't bark (because we value our sanity)

OK, let's be honest, this was my checklist. As far as Tom was concerned – he just wanted a 'proper dog' – you know, one that actually wants to go for a walk.

Belle, our lazy, stubborn Frenchie, looks at you like you've personally offended her if you dare suggest such a thing. Actually get her out, and you'll just be dragging her along like a sack of potatoes.

No, Tom (the original animal lover) wanted a real adventurous, outdoorsy, **proper dog**. Icing on the cake if it's a dog that no-one else would have!

So one Sunday, armed with our list, we called by the local SPA (*Societe Protectrice des Animaux* – essentially France's equivalent to an RSPCA), **just to look**.

After a quick look around, "nothing suitable" I chime heading towards the gate, thinking Tom is right on my heels. No response. I turn.

Tom is kneeling by a cage, talking through the bars. In it, a long-haired German Shepherd is well and truly giving him the puppy eyes. It's ok I think to myself, this isn't the short-haired, small dog we had spoken about.

But before I could remind him of our carefully curated list, he was beckoning over the Manager and asking me to act as translator to his questions.

The woman at the shelter assured us:

- "I have no idea why he would be here, he's such a lovely, gentle dog".
- "Good with people, good with other dogs"
- "The vet thinks he's about 8, not many people want the older dogs" (this of course, was music to Tom's ears)
- "Definitely been a family dog before, not a single accident in the kennels"
- "Never heard him bark"

The final point we now know was a **complete lie**.

Unlike the RSPCA in the UK where, like some reality dating show, you're subjected to an intense interview and a home visit to ensure you're a suitable match. Within the hour of her 'sales pitch', we were driving home with Louis in the back. No time for further discussion. No time to re-think. **Tom was beaming.**

The following day was Monday, so Tom left for work. I decided to work from the kitchen table (as opposed to the office), just to help Louis settle in.

Louis spent the entire day circling me and the dining table as if he was a shark, and I was a seal stranded on an iceberg. He was literally doing laps of the kitchen. I was trying to concentrate on work. Periodically grabbing the laptop to prevent it from flying across the room mid conference call, as he'd take out the power cable clumsily passing by. Agility dog, my ass.

By day 2, he had found his voice. And he clearly had a lot to say. Every imaginary threat required urgent, full-volume barking.

By the time Tom got back from work, I was at breaking point. The house was covered in hair, my nerves were shot, and I was seriously looking through the paperwork for the returns policy.

Over the coming days, weeks (probably months if I'm being honest), things settled down a bit. And if Tom had wanted a proper dog – he got one.

Whilst his back legs aren't the best, if he thinks there's a chance of another walk (even having just finished a 10 mile hike), he's whimpering with excitement and launching himself into the boot like a toddler into a ball pit.

Meanwhile, Belle – witnessing his insanity – will be hiding under the table to avoid her harness going on. Making it abundantly clear that she will not be participating in such nonsense.

But despite the fluff, the barking, and the endless energy. Louis somehow wormed his way into our hearts. He's sensitive, ridiculous and a clumsy liability. But he's ours.

Moral of the story? Never take Tom to a dog shelter.

Whooo Let the Owls Out?

We moved to rural France for the peace and quiet. Or so we thought.

It all began one evening sat outside when we heard a thud and noticed something coming out of the old barn tower shutter at dusk. "Owls!" we gasped. "Actual owls! Nesting! In our barn!"

Cue magical feelings. Rustic pride. Visions of wise woodland creatures hooting softly in the twilight.

Then the babies started screeching.

Not hooting — **screeching**. Like tortured cats trapped in tiny fluffy bodies.

And they do it. All. Night. Long.

Whilst I was googling 'do owls attack' and freaking out every time I needed something from the chest freezer, Tom was in full nature-nerd heaven.

He appointed himself Head Owl Watcher, perching in the garden every evening at dusk, with a beer in one hand, waiting to catch a glimpse.

But it didn't stop with owl watching. Enter: the Merlin app. A bird call recognition tool for people who want to get even nerdier about things that fly.

Merlin listens, analyses, and tells you if you're in the presence of something special, like a rare crested titscratcher (not a real bird, but probably on Tom's wish list).

Now every evening includes Merlin updates.

Tom: "You'll never guess what happened today!"

Me: "What?" thinking some momentous news. A lottery win perhaps?

Tom: "I picked up a red breasted warbler.. Very rare."

Me: "Great."

Tom: "You don't seem excited."

Me: "Because I'm not."

And yet, you somehow get sucked in…

This first year we have

- rescued owls,
- taken in a dehydrated hedgehog
- set up night cameras to catch both *Ragondins (*similar to a beaver*)* and some nesting blue tits feeding their babies.

We named our neighbouring Blue Tits of course. Each after a famous person with initials B.T. such as Belinda Tarlisle & Boris Tohnson. It occupied us for a few evenings, until we realised they were Great Tits so the initial naming thing didn't seem as funny.

The life you once knew in the UK, seems a distant memory. Now you're living in an episode of Springwatch. Living next door to an Owl named Barnaby Keith Whitby Gardner. And with **a man who thinks he is Bill Oddie**.

Language Struggles: The French You Never Learned in School

Press 1 for Panic: Navigating Phone Calls

When I first moved to France, the mere thought of making a phone call in French filled me with dread. I'd meticulously write down what I needed to say, double-check it on Google Translate, and then, before dialling, pray that the person on the other end would stick to my script.

Email quickly became my best friend. It gave me time to think, translate, and avoid the inevitable moment of horror when the conversation veered off course.

Eventually, though, I realised something. Email is great, but in France, many things simply don't get done without a phone call.

The problem with phone calls is that French people respond. And not in slow, easily-structured textbook French, but in full-speed, native French.

And good luck if you get one of those recorded voice greetings with menu options…

Tapez un pour…

Tapez deux pour…

What follows may as well be in Chinese.

You understand so little you get stuck in the dreaded loop, desperately just trying to speak to an actual human.

In the early days, if I absolutely had to call someone, I'd try to plan it out, practicing different ways to say things in case they didn't understand my first attempt. But the second they deviated from the script —game over.

Cue panicked silence, sweats, and a desperate *"désolé, pouvez-vous répéter… plus lentement s'il vous plait?"*

After months of avoidance, I started forcing myself to just pick up the phone. And sure enough, I still stumble through conversations, but at least I don't give myself an anxiety attack before dialling. Progress.

Counting in French – 80 is WHAT?

Learning to count in French starts off as a comforting experience. *Un, deux, trois*, we repeat confidently, feeling like language-learning prodigies. By *soixante-neuf* (69), we're practically bilingual.

Then, like a cruel plot twist, 70 arrives.

Soixante-dix (sixty-ten).

Pardon ?

We blink, assuming we've misheard. But no—this is the moment where French counting stops making sense. 80 (*quatre-vingts*) means four twenties. And 90? *Quatre-vingt-dix* (four twenties and ten). It's as if someone decided numbers were getting boring and needed some flair!

But the real horror begins when you have to use these numbers in real life.

Panic at the Supermarket Checkout

Picture this: you're in a French *supermarché*, confidently placing your cheese and wine (obviously) on the conveyor belt, feeling very *intégré* into French society. The cashier scans everything and casually says, at a million miles per hour, *"Soixante-dix-neuf euros quatre-vingt-cinq."*

You freeze.

Seventy… nine? That's sixty… plus… ten… plus… nine? No, wait, it's just seventy-nine. But what was that other number? Was that eighty-five? Or eighty plus five?

Meanwhile, the queue is growing behind you, mutters of 'stupid engleesh'. A pensioner shifts their weight, probably mentally calculating how much longer they have to live.

By the time you snap back to reality, the cashier is already repeating the number slower, but with the clear undertone of 'we both know you're never going to get this!'

You blindly hand over your bank card despite having a wallet full of cash, just to make the nightmare end.

The phone Number Gauntlet

Then just when you think you've conquered French numbers - you can count to 100 (provided no distractions), you naively attempt to give someone your phone number. In England, this is simple: "o-seven-eight-nine-one-five-nine…"

Not in France.

Here, phone numbers are always spoken in pairs: *zero-sept, cinquante-trois, trente-neuf, quarte-vingt-dix-sept, trente-cinq..* (07 53 39 97 35)

If you say your number as single digits, it transpires the French will physically not be able to write it down until you repeat it correctly.

Desperate to be understood, you attempt the paired format. But halfway through, you panic— forgetting your phone number – you pull out your phone so you can see it.

Once looking at the number, you try again. The French person nods approvingly. You've done it. You feel like you've passed an exam.

Levelling up to Postcodes & the Social Security Number

Then there's the postcodes. My postcode is 17380. Simple, right?

No.

You must say: *dix-sept, trois-cent-quatre-vingt*. (17 – 380)

If you dare to say *un, sept, trois, huit, zero,* the post office worker or government official will stare at you like you just insulted their ancestors.

And if you ever have to give your social security number over the phone? Forget it. It's 15 digits long for gods' sake. By the time you've reached digit six, you've lost track, the person on the other end is sighing dramatically, and you wish you'd just stayed in the UK where numbers make sense.

The truth is, you will never really master French numbers. But that's okay.

Just remember this golden rule: when in doubt, nod, smile, and hand over your *carte bancaire*.

French Words That Sound the Same but Mean Completely Different Things

Learning French is already an uphill battle—the verb conjugations, the gendered nouns, the unspoken pronunciation rules that no one warns you about. But just when you start to feel semi-confident, you realise…

Half the language sounds exactly the same.

It's as if the French took one word, cloned it, gave each clone a different spelling and meaning, and then sat back with a glass of wine, waiting for foreigners to cock-up.

Here's a classic. Imagine you're sitting in a *café*, and someone casually drops the word *ver*. Great, but **which one**?

- *Ver* – **A worm**
- *Vert* – **The color green**
- *Vers* – **Towards**
- *Verre* – **A glass**

So if you say, *"J'ai vu un ver dans un verre vert vers la table"*, congratulations ! You've just said: "I saw a worm in a green glass near the table."

So how are you supposed to understand this?

You're not.

You just guess based on context and hope for the best. Or failing that, just nod and say *"D'accord"*.

A friend, let's call her Sarah, found this out first hand.

At her first-ever French massage, the masseuse asks:

"Ou avez-vous mal ?" (where does it hurt ?)

Wanting to say her neck, she confidently replies:

"Mon Cul"

A raised eyebrow from the masseuse. Because instead of saying *mon cou* (neck) she had just announced she had a sore ass....

The Many Layers of French

French isn't just one language. It's at least five. The way you write to a government official is **wildly** different from how you talk to a neighbour. And somewhere in between, there's a confusing middle ground where you're not sure whether to use "vous" or "tu" and just avoid pronouns altogether.

Let's break it down.

The Very Formal Written Letter (i.e., preparing for battle)

If you've ever tried writing anything formal in French, you'll know that it feels less like crafting a legal document from the 18th century. And if you ever make the mistake of translating it directly into English, you'll sound like you're writing to the Queen.

This is the kind of letter you write to the prefecture, your bank, or anyone who holds terrifying bureaucratic power over your life. It has to sound as though you are humble, eternally grateful, and vaguely terrified.

French version :

"Je me permets de vous adresser la présente afin de solliciter, avec le plus grand respect, votre bienveillance quant à ma demande de rendez-vous, et vous prie d'agréer, Monsieur, Madame, l'expression de mes salutations distinguées."

Literal English translation:

"I am permitting myself to address to you the present letter in order to solicit, with the greatest respect, your benevolence regarding my request for a meeting, and I beg you to accept, Sir, Madam, the expression of my distinguished salutations."

…Seriously… Just to ask for an appointment.

Versus Informal Spoken French (i.e., talking to friends, or a neighbour)

At this point, any formality is gone, words are shortened, and entire chunks of sentences disappear.

French version :

"Ça te dit qu'on se cale un truc ?"

Literal English translation:

"Does it say to you that we slot in a thing?"

…Which somehow translates to: "Wanna make plans?"

At this level, nobody is wasting time on unnecessary words.

In between all of that, you've got anything from still keeping some sentence structure, but dropping the 300-year-old formalities, to polite, but not too direct - the verbal equivalent of tiptoeing into a room, bowing repeatedly, and backing out slowly.

Which 'version' of French you should use, when, is never really clear.

Over the year my French has improved to a point I can eavesdrop outside a café (smug), or so I thought.

Until one day, trying to snoop on some teenagers on the table next to me – I couldn't pick up a thing.

Verlan – Flipping words backward like a secret code (i.e., good luck understanding this one)

I asked my French teacher that week – "ah they're speaking *verlan*" she replied – the world of backward slang – where words get chopped up, and flipped around and suddenly make no sense whatsoever. Fabulous.

Turns out there's a few thousand of these words – that's basically a whole other language!

Maybe I'll just give up now, I thought.

The Power of "D'accord"

One of my earliest and most dangerous French habits was deploying *"D'accord"* when you have no idea.

Didn't catch what they said? *D'accord.*

Didn't even recognise the tense they used? *D'accord.*

They could've been asking if I wanted a receipt or if I consented to signing away my life savings — still *d'accord.*

Tom quickly caught on.

Tom: "So, what did they say?"

Me: "Umm... I think we need to pop back in next week."

Tom: "Why?"

Me: "Unclear. Something about... bringing documents? Or they needed to check with someone? Their dog? Honestly, I got lost after *bonjour.*"

There's a unique kind of adrenaline that comes from saying *"d'accord"* to something you absolutely did not understand, then walking away wondering what you may have just committed to. A minor appointment? A duel at dawn?

I responded *"d'accord"* to a man who was just asking if I wanted a bag once. He looked a bit baffled.

I've since learned to at least throw in a polite *"Pardon, pouvez-vous répéter?"* — but when in doubt, the trusty *"d'accord"* is still there, waiting to either save the day or completely derail it.

Some Days I French, Some Days I... Don't

Some days, I swear, I am Frenching like a pro. I breeze through conversations, throw in the odd French filler word, maybe a casual subjunctive.

There was one day I caught myself casually making small talk with the postman.

He handed me a parcel, made some comment about the weather changing, and before I could stop myself, I nodded and hit him with a *bah oui* (well yes). He carried on, so I doubled down with an *oh là là là là*—delivered with just the right amount of dramatic exasperation.

It wasn't until I shut the door that it hit me. I hadn't just blagged my way through the conversation—I'd nailed it.

No awkward silences, no panicked nodding, no desperate glances at the door.

Honestly, I inwardly gave myself a high-five and practically felt ready to apply for a passport.

And then... there are the other days.

Days when I open my mouth, and my brain panics, launching me into an incomprehensible **mix of Franglais**.

Days when I forget the word for 'yesterday' (*hier*, I know this!) and instead describe it as "the day before today."

Days when someone asks me a simple question—like if I want a receipt—and I freeze like a deer in headlights, mumble "*oui*" (which was not the right answer), and then walk away with a very unnecessary receipt.

Worst of all is when I attempt a casual, confident exchange and then immediately regret it. The other day, a woman asked me if I lived in the village. A normal question. Simple. I should've said, *oui, j'habite ici*. Instead, I panicked and said *je suis une maison*—which means "I am a house."

She nodded slowly and backed away. Probably for the best.

But that's the beauty of learning French in France. Some days, you're flying. Other days, you're crashing. And occasionally, **you're a house**.

Parlez-Vous Del Boy?

I was told by my teacher not to stress too much about pronunciation. That the French find English people speaking French just as endearing as we find French people speaking English.

You know, the way we all collectively swoon when a French person says something like, "Eet ees not ze same", or "I sink eet will rain today."

Somehow, though, it doesn't feel quite the same when the roles are reversed.

There's something quite special about hearing an English person butcher the French language with **absolutely zero effort**.

For example, at the vets the other day. A woman entered and proudly announced "BOND-JORE!" to the receptionist like she'd just stepped off the set of Only Fools and Horses. Or the ones who, upon realising their French is non-existent, switch to English but speak reeeeally sloooowly and LOUDLY, because apparently stretching out the words and shouting them will make them magically understood.

"I... WOULD... LIKE... A... COFFEE... PLEASE."

Look, no one's expecting you to sound like a Parisian newsreader. We're all just trying our best here. But I do believe throwing in a bit of effort goes a long way. I've found a half-decent *bonjour* (without the hard 'jore' at the end obviously) and a *merci* with a vaguely correct 'r' can do wonders.

Culture & Traditions: Embracing the French Way

The local market – A weekly ritual

There's something undeniably magical about a French market.

The moment you arrive you're hit by the buzz – locals greeting each other with double kisses (*la bise*); stallholders engaging with their customers; delicious smells. The old boys nursing their morning *Ricard*, and the faint sounds of Edith Pilaf playing from a speaker.

Of course you grab a table at the busiest *café* terrace for some people watching. Order a hot chocolate. Or a glass of wine. **No-one will judge**, and it's somewhere past breakfast.

The stalls: a feast for the senses

- Fresh seafood: Bright pink crevettes & langoustines, oysters shucked in front of you.
- A rainbow of fresh vegetables
- Succulent cuts of meat and enormous slabs of *pâté*
- *Artisan boulangers* selling golden baguettes, flaky buttery croissants, and *pattisseries* showcasing cakes and tartes so beautiful that you feel guilty for eating them.
- The unmistakeable aroma of rotisserie chicken, spinning slowly, the juices dripping onto the potatoes below.
- A token Asian stall deep frying some crispy nems, because even in rural France, you sometimes need a break from the cheese.
- Seasonal treasures like glossy chestnuts, juicy olives or wild garlic.

It's no surprise the French, young or old, are often wheeling a chariot (trolley) behind them – they know it's impossible to leave empty handed.

The best 6 euros I ever spent

These markets aren't just for food. There are vendors selling clothes, wicker baskets, handbags, even mattresses.

Which brings me onto the single most useful kitchen tool I've ever bought. It's like a mini food processor, but manually operated by a pull chord. A few tugs and boom – finely diced onions, garlic, herbs whatever you need. I bartered her down to 6 euros – money well spent to prevent onion tears ever again. Highly recommend.

Beware those free samples

Of course not every market experience passes without a hitch.

On one occasion, I had my mum in tow. We were at the Saturday market in my local town, picking up something special for dinner.

We were passing a *charcuterie* stall, when the vendor handed us a piece to try. Obligingly we popped it into our mouths, and as we went to chew he said one word that made our stomachs drop.

"*Cheval*"

Horse.

Now I'm fairly open minded about food. Will try everything once. But there's something about finding out mid-chew that you're eating black beauty's cousin.

Swallow, don't think. Swallow don't think.

We learnt the hard way that day to ask a few questions before greedily diving into the free samples.

But every week the market is the same. Despite coming in 'for a few essentials', you will always leave with enough food to feed a small village, and admiration for the French and their ability to turn a grocery shop into an experience, and maybe a little bit tipsy from your wine too.

Pétanque – More Than Just Boules

1907 in the south of France someone was playing a similar game to Petanque and thought it was way too much effort, so they invented this version where you stand still - **a sport invented on basis of doing less? Truly French genius.**

Every French village has it's *pétanque* court, usually in a shady spot. Walk past in the summer, and you'll see a group of older men – often wearing flat caps and smoking, leisurely engaged in **a slow, but intense competition.**

There's always at least one chap, arms crossed, shaking his head in disappointment.

It's not just a casual way for old guys to pass the time, it's **practically a religion**.

Of course, it's not just for pensioners, Tom and I will often partake in a friendly-game (when in Rome and all that!). Calling it friendly is however incredibly misleading.

Now we play by the French rules of course.

Drinking while playing, whilst not officially required is **practically mandatory**.

If there is even a fraction of a doubt about which ball is closer, you can expect one of us to be pulling out the string. **Arguing over millimetres is par for the course.**

What usually happens. I line up my shot, land it beautifully right next to the jack (*cochonnet*, as the French call it), feeling very pleased with myself.

Only for Tom to brutally smash my ball out of the way with a strong shot. Every. Single. Time.

Now knocking other players balls out of the way, is not considered unsporting here. In fact, it's deemed tactical genius. Just not if you're on the other end of it, clearly.

Thus the game usually ends with one of us (me) storming off in frustration, swearing we're never playing again.. until next weekend.

14th July the most important day in the French Calendar.

The 14th July is Toms Birthday – it just also happens to be *Bastille Day*.

This is "French Independence Day"—a day of fireworks, celebrations, and general *joie de vivre*.

Before making the move to France, my mum and I spent Bastille Day weekend in La Rochelle. We had a lovely time soaking in the buzzy summer atmosphere, and as night fell, crowds gathered along the harbour, everyone eagerly waiting. And then—it began. A dazzling firework display launched from the water between La Rochelle's two iconic towers, lighting up the sky. It was, without a doubt, one of the best fireworks displays I had ever seen.

Our First Bastille Day in France: A Pique-Nique of course.

Fast forward to our first July 14th as official French residents, and we were determined to make it memorable. My mum was visiting, Tom's parents had come down too, and we decided to hire a boat and cruise up the Charente River, passing stunning *châteaux* that look straight out of a fairy tale. It was peaceful, relaxing… very French indeed.

Obviously, we had to stop for a *'pique-nique'*. Most relaxing until some curious cattle got a little 'too close'.

Now, a French picnic is no ordinary affair. The French take picnicking **very seriously**.

You'll often see entire families gathered in an *aire* (picnic spot), but they're not just sitting on the grass with a meal deal from E-Leclerc. *Non, non, non.* They've got:

- **A trestle table** (*bien sur!* Because who picnics without one?)
- **A tablecloth** (obviously)
- **Real glasses** (plastic cups ? *Quelle horreur !*)
- What appears to be **at least three courses**
- **Wine.** Always wine.

They're not just having lunch. They are **profiting** of course!

And if you ever need proof that food and lunch is sacred in France, you'll enjoy this story. Some friends in town over lunchtime passed a parked work van with some builders inside. Now, in England, this would mean:

- 3 blokes, sitting in the front seats of van
- Scoffing a Greggs pasty
- Possibly a cup of tea in a thermos

In France?

- A full dining table setup inside the back of the van
- Complete with a tablecloth (yes in a work van!), cutlery & plates
- A bottle of red wine (because, of course)

They were sat, eating a proper meal and chatting away like they were in a Parisian bistro.

Strikes: A National Past Time

France the land of rich culture, exquisite cuisine and… **perpetual strikes**.

Returning from the UK one day, I had a lucky escape. My 5 hour drive could have taken 4x that, had I not narrowly missed the wall of tractors blocking the motorways. *Sacrebleu*!

The French farmers were thinking what better way to voice the grievances of lower incomes and increased regulation than by turning the motorways into a car park for their machinery! Why not.

Then there was the Baguette strike in 2023 around the growing cost of ingredients. The Boulangers stopped production for a day – making it nearly impossible for anyone to get a baguette – you can imagine the uproar! Dough-lightful.

The Cheese and Wine strike, which to be fair looked more like a social gathering. Less 'down with the system' and more 'up with the *pique-nique*'. Who knew advocating for workers' rights could be so fun?

However, my favourite strike has to be the '*Je Chie Dans La Seine*', which translates to 'I poop in the Seine,

The French were clearly not too pleased about the government's €1.4 billion scheme to clean up the River Seine for the 2024 Olympics. With news that President Macron would be taking a dip to prove how clean it was, this prompted a plan in protest of the spending, to do just that.

Take a poo. In the Seine.

Toilet cubicles were installed under the cover of darkness along the river banks in Paris. Someone even set up a website which calculated the water flow from surrounding towns – if you wanted to partake you could do your business 50 miles away, knowing it would arrive safely in Paris at the right time for Macrons swim. Genius.

But despite the strikes, life in France carries on with a '*Je Ne Sais Quoi*'.

There is often a degree of sympathy with the strikers – or even **solidarity.** Trains may stop, baguettes may be scarce, but the French remain unfazed. A testament to the national ethos. When life gives you lemons – make a nice *citron pressé*.

Strikes are more than just disruptions, whilst they have a deep meaning, they are often infused with creativity and humour showing **rebellion and French spirit**. Maybe now we're at the heart of why I feel so at home here.

Apéros: The Best French Invention

Our first *apéro* in France was a lesson in the fine art of *joie de vivre*.

We'd been invited, by one of Toms customers, for what we assumed to be "a quick drink and some nibbles".

You know, **something light** – a glass of wine, some olives and a bit of bread perhaps.

Our host had other ideas. It was in fact a full-blown ***apéro dinatoire***, a sneaky French tradition where "pre-dinner drinks" turns into an entire meal – 7 hours of eating, drinking, and trying to count the courses.

It started around 6pm, which is the unofficial start of *l'heure de l'apéro* – where the French down tools, and turn their attention to more important matters: wine, snacks and conversation.

Our host welcomed us with a glass of wine, and a tray of *amuse-bouches*. Followed by some *crudités* – little sticks of carrot, cucumber and bread served with a dip. Olives of course – which appear to be absolutely mandatory for any *apéro*.

Then the charcuterie comes out– wafer thin slices of *saucisson*, with *pâté*. An array of crackers and crispy things emerges from the kitchen. And just when you're thinking you've got to be nearly done, the cheeseboard arrives.

Did you know the French dedicate an entire supermarket aisle to *apéro*. snacks? This country takes its pre-dinner grazing very seriously.

The drinks flow continuously throughout of course, and by the time dessert shows up you feel like you may need to be rolled home.

We sat around that table, eating, drinking, chatting, laughing. The whole thing wrapped up for us around 1am.

That's the thing about *apéro* culture – it's not just about the food. It's the whole experience. It embodies the French art of living – that it's something that should be savoured.

So whilst *apéro* might technically mean a quick drink before dinner, don't always be fooled. If you hear the words ***apéro dinatoire***, **pace yourself.** Because you're in for a long night!

The Brocante: A journey from obsession to restraint

When I first discovered the world of French *brocantes*, it was like stepping into a universe where everything looked like something you'd buy from a shabby chic etsy account, perfect for my new French home.

There is **zero** comparison to the UKs car boot sale.

Inevitably, I became obsessed. The allure of uncovering some hidden treasure was irresistible.

At first, I never left a *brocante* empty-handed. Oh no.

Whether it was some pewter jars, or a painted jug, I bought it all. Some items may have been questionably useful, but I told myself, "It's the charm of it!". But there came a point— when I was moaning about how much crap we have—that I had to rein it in. Our house began to resemble a small antique shop, and not a particularly well-organised one. Given I'd always been into a minimalist interiors and style this was quite the change.

I heard of a 'big *brocante*' happening in Brouage, a citadel near Rochefort on the South West coast (about 30 mins from home), and it was on my day off! I would be there, and Belle would come with me – girls day out.

It was a maze of treasures, 100's of vendors and stools to get lost in for hours – even with my new-found restraint, I was still tempted.

However, *brocantes* I quickly learnt are a scent paradise for a dog. All these old things taken out of peoples' homes and attics were lining the street. Every 10 steps took 10 minutes as I dragged her away from snorting and snuffling at everything from a vintage typewriter, to a large framed

18th century portrait of someone's great-grandmother (praying the latter wouldn't be chosen by Belle as a good place to relieve herself!)

And then disaster strikes. Picture it: I was happily wandering past a particularly charming *brocante* stall, quite taken by a beautiful *coffre* (chest/truck) that definitely needed to come home with me. I had this vision for my outdoor entertaining area - the *coffre* would be used to store some blankets and the mosquito candles (an essential for summer time in France). It was perfect!

The vendor picked up on my interest, an incoming sale he was thinking! But then it hit me—I had no cash. None. Literally Zero. How did I forget to check for money before setting off to the market of a lifetime? What a rookie!

I stood there for a good minute, still pretending to be absorbed in the *coffre* and then in a flash I scarpered, defeated, and empty-handed—apart from a newfound appreciation for always double-checking my wallet before heading to a *brocante*.

Fête de la Musique: When the French Take the Party to the Streets

If there's one thing the French do well—aside from bread, cheese, and striking—it's turning absolutely anything into a reason for a street party. And *Fête de la Musique* is proof of that.

Every year on June 21st, entire towns and villages transform into open-air music festivals. From professional bands to slightly **questionable karaoke enthusiasts**, anyone with an instrument (or, in some cases, just a microphone and a dream) takes to the streets. It's like Glastonbury, if Glastonbury had more accordions and fewer wellies.

We went to our first *Fête de la Musique* thinking it would be a few musicians on a stage somewhere. Oh no. Every corner had its own setup—drummers in the town square, a rock band outside the *boulangerie*, a jazz trio next to a *charcuterie*. It was as if the entire country had collectively decided to turn the streets into their personal concert venues.

By 9 p.m., the entire town was buzzing. People of all ages spilled out of bars and restaurants, dancing, singing, and generally having a great time. Small children ran around with no intention of going to bed, elderly couples swayed along to whatever music was closest, and groups of teenagers lurked around looking effortlessly cool.

Of course, the French don't do a night out without wine in hand, so every available surface became a makeshift bar. Plastic cups of *rosé* and *bière pression* were clutched by nearly everyone, and the idea of just popping out for a quiet drink had long gone out the window.

By midnight, some bands were still going, some had clearly abandoned their setlists, and some had just given up and joined the crowd. We staggered home, ears ringing, slightly wobbly, and already marking next year's *Fête de la Musique* on the calendar.

The French may have a reputation for being a little reserved, but give them a *Fête* and a bit of live music, and they'll party in the street like it's the last night on Earth.

A Spooky Night of Confusion

Halloween in France seems to be getting more popular, but thankfully, it's not quite reached American levels yet.

No inflatable skeletons taking over front lawns, no houses dripping in fake cobwebs, and—so far—no one knocking on your door expecting a full-sized chocolate bar.

But there are some places embracing the spirit, and one of them just so happened to be *Château de Crazannes*, one of our closest and most intriguing *château*.

A Chance to Have a Nose Around

The *château* isn't usually open to the public, except for special events like weddings. We'd admired it plenty of times from the outside—rubber necking whilst walking by with the dogs.

So, when I saw a Halloween event advertised on Facebook, I thought:

1. Why not? Something different!

2. Finally, a chance to have a proper nose around inside.

It really is amazing the activities you sign yourself up for when you're living in rural France, I tell you. Refer to earlier chapter re. needing a hobby.

We had no idea what to expect but assumed some decorations, maybe a few pumpkins, and a bit of light-hearted spookiness.

When we arrived, the *château* was all lit up in eerie colours, looking every bit the haunted house. So far, so good.

Everyone—and I mean everyone—was in full fancy dress.

We? Were not.

This already put us at **a distinct social disadvantage**.

Still, we powered through.

We were swiftly ushered into a group of fellow guests—all French—and told that we would be solving a mystery.

This was not what we had signed up for.

If there's one thing more terrifying than a haunted *château*, it's being thrown into a complex game of mystery and riddles in a foreign language.

There were actors playing different roles, leading us from room to room—the servants' kitchen, the grand dining hall, the chapel, the drawing room.

Each place revealed new clues and suspicious characters, and the group was deep in discussion, throwing out theories.

Meanwhile, we were… nodding along enthusiastically.

Attempting to Participate.

Tom, ever the problem solver, suggested an approach.

"Let's just watch everyone else and copy what they do."

Incroyable.

So we're hunting around a large drawing room, opening drawers, and moving things around – with no idea what we're actually looking for.

Someone asked me a question.

I panicked. Responded *"D'accord."*

Which, to be clear, made absolutely no sense in the context.

After an hour of pretending to understand what was happening, we subtly started edging towards the exit. It probably took us an another 30 minutes of awkwardness to find the right moment to get away.

Whilst the mystery remained unsolved, we got our nose around the *château*—which, let's be honest, was all we really wanted in the first place.

Lesson Learned? If you're putting yourself in a situation where you must have a good level of French to survive, **always have an exit strategy**.

Gone Fishin'...

The *carrelets* – those charming wooden fishing huts on stilts, along the Atlantic coast. Dangling huge square-shaped nets into the water, serving as both functional fishing apparatus and picturesque landmarks. Traditionally, fishermen lower these expansive nets into the water, and wait for the tide, before hoisting them back up (hopefully with a bountiful catch!)

Tom, with his love of the outdoors, is a keen angler. So naturally, we decided to rent one for the afternoon. Give it a go.

Armed with all the gear (and precisely none of the idea), we brought sardines, tuna, and enough fish oil to deep fry a whale.

I'd read somewhere that this would "attract the big ones." Instead, it attracted… **absolutely nothing.** Not even an inquisitive crab.

Operating the *carrelet* net is hilariously manual. There's a giant winch, ropes that tangle easily, and the subtle fear that you're going to drop something important into the estuary.

We took turns heaving the net up and down like it was a medieval drawbridge, fully expecting the net to be weighed down with our haul.

We did get some seaweed. And at one point… a stick.

Eventually, we caught a handful of tiny fish. **Like, really tiny**. The sort of fish that would get bullied in an aquarium.

All in all, we spent hours hauling, baiting, waiting, and wildly overestimating our chances. But with a beer in hand, the sun setting, it was hard to be disappointed.

The fish may have been small, but our spirits? High.

It turns out *carrelet* fishing is 90% waiting (and drinking a beer), 9% hoping (and drinking a beer), and 1% pretending you meant to catch that twig.

Joyeux Noël: Mice, Mayhem & the Great Lindt Heist

Christmas in France is a little different.

You don't spend most of December at Christmas Parties, jigging around to the Pogues, and giving your liver a bashing in preparation for the real thing.

Flashing hats and Christmas jumpers are reserved for the privacy of your own home. Even in rural France (where things like crocs even seem to be acceptable), the French would not be seen dead in them.

There are no hyped-up nieces and nephews tearing through wrapping paper like a pack of feral elves. Whilst *Père Noël* exists in France, he does so in a far more **understated way**.

No cheap crackers with terrible jokes that my Mum and Auntie Susie seem to find 'roll around on the floor' and almost 'pee your pants' hilarious.

One might say Christmas in France is a little more *'civilisé'*.

France do excel in Christmas Markets – You can expect twinkling lights and some artisan stalls selling handmade wicker baskets, local delicacies such as *foie gras* and the obligatory *vin chaud*. A stall selling huitres of course, shucked on spot. As nothing says 'festive spirit' quite like slurping down a raw oyster in the freezing cold!

For our first Christmas living in France we had good company (hosting Tom's parents), good food (mostly thanks to Toms mum), good wine (of course) —and an uninvited guest.

Christmas Eve: The Seafood Extravaganza

Now, in the UK, Christmas Eve usually involves last-minute panic shopping, frantically peeling potatoes, and a regrettable pub session.

In France ? *Le réveillon de Noël*, Christmas Eve, is for feasting.

Enter: *Un plateau de Fruits de Mer*. **The Seafood Platter**.

You usually pre-order your platter from the local fishmonger (within the supermarket). On the days running up to Christmas they will put up a board with some options to choose from. A Pick'n'Mix of seafood! You order what you want and what time you want to collect it, and *voilà*.

Presented on a beautiful platter, on a bed of ice – a mountain of oysters, plump langoustines, crevettes, lobster, crab. The French don't mess around when it comes to seafood. It's extravagant. It's delicious. And exactly the kind of Christmas tradition I can get behind.

The Snow House: A Christmas Tradition (and Rodent Hotel)

For a bit of fun, we adopted a tradition courtesy of my Auntie Lauren – the Snow House.

Now this is a very sophisticated take on a Christmas lucky dip—-aka a cardboard box, lovingly decorated with a snowy roof, cut-out windows and doors (because we are *artistes*), filled with cheap but useful gifts from Action or Temu. Think: novelty socks, candles, torches, and the ever-classy Donald Trump toilet paper.

It had been waiting for its unveiling in the office. One evening, hearing some rustling, something felt… off.

"I think we might have mice Tom."

Tom, ever the sceptic, sighed and picked up the Snow House. And at that very moment, as if perfectly scripted for a Christmas horror film, a tiny mouse poked its head out of the window.

I screamed. Tom flung the box onto the floor, and our uninvited house guest scuttled away behind the desk.

Once the adrenaline had subsided, we inspected the damage. The Snow House, it turned out, had been hosting an all-you-can-eat chocolate buffet. The fancy Lindt truffles? Gone. The chocolate orange after eights? Vanished. The wrappers? Shredded into festive confetti.

It was a full-scale Christmas crime scene, complete with tiny teeth marks.

This, apparently, is what happens when you try to bring festive joy to what is basically an old barn in rural France. You get a **rodent infestation**.

Whilst the chocolates may have met a tragic end, we still had a wonderful time.

Christmas in France is all about indulgence, tradition, and apparently—uninvited wildlife. Next year, the Snow House is getting reinforced.

Final Thoughts: Are You Sure You Want to Stay?

The top 3 things I miss about the UK

1. Friends & Family: Bienvenue Chez-Nous

One of the biggest fears about moving to another country is missing family and friends—the casual pop-in for a cup of tea, the ease of seeing people without a forward plan.

And obviously, I miss my friends and family terribly at times. Winter in rural France can also be a bit… drab. There's a reason the shutters are closed and everyone hibernates from November to March. But the moment the first daffodil dares to bloom, something predictable happens.

Your phone starts pinging.

"Heyyy, how's France? Just wondering what you're up to mid-May… June… actually, all of July?"

The truth? The moment you move abroad, your home becomes a free B&B.

It starts with one set of visitors. Then another. Then suddenly, you're running **an unofficial guesthouse**, complete with endless washing of towels and bedding, and airport pickups.

In our first year alone, we had 28 visitors (or 31 if you count my mum's three visits). She's even taken to leaving a wardrobe of clothes here for next time.

By the time August rolls around, you start wondering if you should have just gone into the *gîte* business properly – which would have made the visa application easier after all.

Of course these visitors get the full French initiation immersion package:

- *Apéros* on arrival. (Mandatory.)
- Whistle-stop sightseeing tours. (Because that's just what I do best.)
- More cheese, wine and seafood than they thought physically possible.
- An unfortunate tendency to leave with minor injuries (turns out painted wooden stairs + wet feet + several bottles of *rosé* = disaster).

They may arrive fresh-faced and excited, but they leave in need of a detox, a lie-down, and possibly some paracetamol.

So if you're reading this because you're debating the move and worried about missing friends and family—don't be. In the world today, there's always facetime and whatsapp to keep us digitally connected. And if they're anything like my lot, they'll **sniff out a cheap holiday** in seconds.

So really, the question isn't "Will I be lonely?" It's "Do I have enough towels for the next wave of visitors?"

Then there are a few other home comforts I miss.. Which are of course food related

2. Cadburys Chocolate.

This just **doesn't exist in France**. The chocolate here is just not the same - And I will happily share this debate with a chocolatier if necessary. Thankfully, that persistent flow of visitors helps to keep my stash going. The very least they can do in exchange for the hospitality of course!

3. A Carvery.

Now France have some of the best restaurants in the world, but on those cold winter Sundays, I dream of being in that queue. Holding your warm plate excitedly. Eyeing up the huge variety of hearty goodness that awaits, with zero peeling and cooking effort. Slices of different juicy meats, roast potatoes, broccoli cheese, hell a Yorkshire **and** some pigs and blankets too.... Just pile as much as you can on, and smother it in a thick gravy.... Yum.

The top 3 things I'll never give up about France

1. The Ultimate Choose-Your-Own-Adventure

The first thing I really love about living in France? It's massive. No, really—coming from the UK, where a "long drive" means anything over two hours, the sheer scale and variety of France still amazes me, and provides endless opportunities for adventures in our campervan.

Fancy a weekend in Paris? Easy.

A ski trip to the Alps or Pyrenees? Just throw your gear in the car.

Wine tasting in Burgundy? Weekend trip.

A Christmas market in Annecy? Why not.

A road trip to Croatia? Been there, done that.

Côte d'Azur for some yacht-gawking and posh dining? Yes please.

And the best part? No airport stress, no faffing with liquid allowances or baggage fees—just jump in the car and go.

The toll roads might not be thrilling, but they're quiet, efficient, and get you where you need to be. Even Spain is an easy day trip—just a quick hop over the border, no fuss.

France practically begs you to explore it. Free water points, loads of aires, and endless scenic spots to park up overnight. Whether it's mountains, beaches, vineyards, or medieval villages, adventure is always just a drive away.

2. Sunshine and Sitting Outside

One of the biggest perks of life in France? The sheer outdoorsiness of it all.

Not in an extreme survivalist way—no one's fashioning clothes from wild bore hind, or making shoes out of tree bark (although I suspect Tom wishes we were). But in the why-would-you-ever-sit-inside kind of way.

Evenings stretch on forever, with the sun politely refusing to set at a reasonable hour. The temperature doesn't drop, so every dinner is alfresco.

We eat outside, we drink outside, we sit outside bars and restaurants watching the world go by.

Spring and autumn often throw in a good few weeks of surprise summer, so you'll find yourself sitting on a terrace in March or October, t-shirt and shorts, sunglasses on,

With all this sunshine, plans rarely get rained off. Dog walks, bike rides around the vineyards, paddleboarding or kayaking on the Charente —France practically forces you into a more active lifestyle, purely because it's too nice to stay indoors.

And then there's August—wall-to-wall sunshine, scorching (and I mean scorching) days. A month of pure, undisturbed, solar-powered laziness with a limb dipped in water at all times.

And finally..

3. **Life in the slow lane: Where everyday feels like a holiday**

Back in the UK, life felt like a constant sprint – always somewhere to be, something to do and never quite enough time to do it.

If there's one thing the French have mastered, it's the art of not being in a hurry.

At first, I found this **infuriating**. I spent my first few months in France wondering why I couldn't just get things done. And **absolutely no chance between the hours of 12-2pm**.

But the more time you spend here, the more you realise it's not about slowness—it's about presence and *profiter*.

Take the concept of waiting your turn. Whether in a supermarket or pharmacy, people acknowledge each other's existence. If someone behind you has just a baguette and a bottle of wine (which is half of France, at any given moment), you let them go ahead with a quick *allez-y*. They'll be profusely grateful, there'll be a lot of *merci, c'est gentil*, and you'll feel like a saint.

The biggest contrast for me is balancing this lifestyle with my very unrelaxed corporate job. One moment, I'm on a video call discussing "high-priority escalations" and "urgent deadlines". The next, I'm in town, where the biggest drama of the day is whether the *boulangerie* still has any *pain suisse*. It's like living in two different time zones (literally). And I finally understand the meaning of 'work-life balance'.

Over time, I've come to appreciate the slower pace. To kick-back and enjoy the moment. In fact, it still almost feels like I'm on a **permanent holiday**.

Yes, it can still be frustrating when you just want to get something done. But there's something charming about a country where a lunch break is sacred, conversations aren't rushed, and kindness in everyday moments is just a part of life.

The moment you realise you've accidentally become a little bit French

There was a time when the very idea of my visa expiring would have sent me into full-blown panic mode. But somehow along the way, I've gone a bit... French about it all.

I was ready for this. Paperwork? Check. Copies of paperwork? Check. Copies of copies, because I know how this goes? Check. Ready to renew online well ahead of time. But of course, the system had other ideas. My visa type couldn't be renewed online.

Pas possible.

I had to go to the prefecture in person. Fine. No problem.

Booked an appointment at my local prefecture, where they essentially just logged me into the same website I'd already tried and looked genuinely surprised when it didn't work. Their advice? I needed to go to La Rochelle instead.

So I booked another appointment, another day trip to La Rochelle. A stack of paperwork in hand, I sat down with the official who methodically checked everything and – miraculously – confirmed I had all the right documents. Success! But instead of handing me my *titre de séjour* (residency card), they handed me a temporary document extending my visa until the end of April. *Pas de problème,* they said. You'll receive a text when its ready.

Whilst the old me would have panicked – I was returning to the UK in a few weeks – would this slip of paper work? I just shrugged and thought *ça va aller* (it'll be ok).

No daily chasing of the prefecture, no scouring the expat groups and having sleepless nights based on their horror stories – nope I had faith in the charmingly inefficient maze that is French administration.

Sure enough, one day six months later – completely unprompted - and only six months late – I finally got the SMS to book the appointment to collect my *titre de séjour*.

And that's when it hit me – I've gone full *c'est la vie*. The system does work.. **eventually.** And the trick is learning to trust it. Even when your visa has technically expired.

So I'm in. Well, **at least for another year.**

We came to France for the dream, we stayed for the lifestyle, and somehow we've ended up a little bit French.

Surviving Year One has been a roller coaster of a ride – but I wouldn't change a thing - baguettes bureaucracy and all.

The end.

Printed in Dunstable, United Kingdom